A SAFARI IN THE EQUITY WORLD

Ritesh Dhoot is an investment professional in a global multi-asset investment firm and is responsible for its research and intelligence functions. Before this, he has worked with Deutsche Bank and JP Morgan in the UK and India respectively. He has an MBA from Management Development Institute (MDI), Gurgaon, India, and holds a Chartered Financial Analyst charter and a Financial Risk Manager certificate. He lives and works in the UAE and has been a long-only investor in Indian equity markets for a good part of the last two decades.

A SAFARI IN THE EQUITY WORLD

RITESH DHOOT

RUPA

Published by
Rupa Publications India Pvt. Ltd 2019
7/16, Ansari Road, Daryaganj
New Delhi 110002

Sales Centres:
Allahabad Bengaluru Chennai
Hyderabad Jaipur Kathmandu
Kolkata Mumbai

Copyright © Ritesh Dhoot 2019

The views and opinions expressed in this book are the author's own and the facts are as reported by him, and the publishers are not in any way liable for the same. The author is not a SEBI registered Research Analyst. All readers are advised to seek the services of competent professionals in the field of personal finance and investments and are also advised to independently evaluate the information/insights and market conditions/risks involved before making any investment decision. Neither the author nor the publisher shall be liable for any damages whether direct or indirect, incidental, special or consequential including lost revenue or lost profits that may arise from or in connection with the use of the information contained in this book.

ISBN: 978-93-5333-705-6

First impression 2019

10 9 8 7 6 5 4 3 2 1

Printed at Replika Press Pvt. Ltd, Sonepat

This book is sold subject to the condition that it shall not,
by way of trade or otherwise, be lent, resold, hired out, or otherwise
circulated, without the publisher's prior consent, in any form of binding
or cover other than that in which it is published.

CONTENTS

Introduction	vii
1. The Bear Came First	1
2. Lion's Opportunity—Can Catch Them All	19
3. Kori Bustard's Feather—Trigger for Investment Action	25
4. Frozen Flamingo—Sector in Distress	41
5. Dolphin Mud-Net—Befriend Uncertainty	60
6. City Monkeys—Finding Manna in a New Territory	79
7. Starling Murmurations—Clone a Web of Investors	94
8. Black Heron's Umbrella—Uniquely Designed to Compete	107
9. Hachi Dog—Consistently Loyal to His Owner	121
10. Bacteria's Evolution—Unstoppable Innovation	133
11. Green Heron's Trick—Promoter Baits Investors	139
12. Principles—To Become a Better Investor	154
13. To Forecast Indian Markets, Analyse the US Markets	169
Acknowledgments	173
Notes	174

INTRODUCTION

A good impression is sort of a juxtaposition of disparate elements.

—Kate McKinnon, American actress

My safari trip to Kenya triggered the conceptualization of this book.

In August 2012, we landed at the Nairobi airport, all excited and looking forward to our first wildlife adventure. On the afternoon of the fourth day, an hour passed anxiously waiting to witness the migration of wildebeests of the Masai Mara National Reserve. The wildebeests went back and forth but they could not muster up the courage to jump into the water and cross the Mara River to make the journey famously known as the great migration. Deadwood was floating, which the pack probably mistook for a crocodile. Finally, the wildebeest at the head of the pack took a leap of faith. Social proof set in and the whole pack followed, one by one, jumping into the water, knowing there is safety in numbers. And we sprang into action, with our cameras clicking, from the pop-out roof of our car. Just as the first wildebeest reached midway, a crocodile emerged from nowhere and grabbed it by its neck. After a few minutes of struggle for its survival, the wildebeest gave in.

It was rare for tourists to witness an attack and I felt lucky to be part of it. However, I cannot say that I enjoyed it. Instead, the moment shocked me and awakened my analytical mind. I began to question where that wildebeest went wrong. To me, it was the *first mover disadvantage*, otherwise observed in the corporate world, while venturing into uncharted territory, but set in the wild. Since then, I could not stop comparing the wild to the investment world.

The trip was supposed to disconnect me from my investing routine. On the contrary, it pushed me even closer to both—investing and the wilderness. Upon returning from my trip, I immersed myself into the study of animal behaviour. I intended to unearth unique investment themes and strategies, and understand the investing world through a different lens. Everything from animals' hunting to survival strategies found my attention. The research yielded various animal strategies, which had astonishing similarities to the investment themes I was already practising. These analogies made sense; as in the animal kingdom and the corporate world the fittest survives. Studying the wild offers a rich understanding of corporations and equity markets. I also discovered many novel and interesting wildlife analogies that remain elusive to the investor communities. Perhaps, ethologists never took investment seriously and similarly, few investors ever took the time to go to the wild.

This book pinpoints investment themes with an aim to reassure investors to decisively invest when they come across opportunities that resemble one of these themes. These themes are broadly defined, as opposed to being very narrow, making them reasonably exhaustive. In my investing career, most of the investment ideas that I came across would neatly fit into one of these illustrated themes. Additionally, broad investment themes, unlike one or a few tightly defined themes, allow investors to adapt to the current realities of the system. As renowned investor, Howard Mark wrote in his book, *The Most Important Thing*, 'I most want to emphasize is how essential it is that one's investment approach be intuitive and adaptive rather than be fixed and mechanistic'.

These themes have universal application and thus can benefit equity investors in any part of the world. However, as I practise investing in the Indian equity markets, most of the examples and stock picks associated with these themes are taken from Indian markets. You might consider skipping these Indian stock examples if they are not your focus area. These stock picks highlight why they were compelling when I bought them. This approach serves a dual purpose. One, it educates the reader and can be used as a case study; two, it calls for action when an investor encounters similar circumstances in the future.

I wrote this book for three types of readers, and I dedicate the book to each of them. First, to the general reader who has a reasonable understanding of the corporate and financial world and its terminologies. To suit his taste, I have tried to keep the book free of technical and financial terms as much as possible, as Albert Einstein put it, 'Everything must be made as simple as possible, but no simpler.' The writing style, thus, is a tight ropewalk, whereby I have simplified the writing to the extent possible so as to not dilute the content and message. The chapters in the book should read like short tales of the financial world. Analogies to the animal kingdom are sprinkled across the book to add spice to the reading. I hope that these will provoke some to review the analogies, and further build on them.

The second reader who I am dedicating this book to is an investment expert. He is the toughest to please. I hope that he will find some of the investment themes new. The associated stock examples should provide him with fresh perspectives on why some companies have done so well. The analogy with the animal kingdom should make each theme an exciting read and strengthen his conviction of its prospects. Perhaps, it would instil the zeal to look at familiar themes differently, or come up with entirely new themes. Alternatively, it may motivate him enough to pen down his investing experience in a book.

My third imaginary reader is the finance and investment student. For him, the book is organized and structured to allow easy assimilation of various investment themes which have been proven to work repeatedly in the market. The analogy with the animal kingdom portrays how disparate things are interrelated, and possibly should stimulate him to identify more analogies—between markets, industries and other unrelated fields. For the student who is still not able to make up his mind about investing as a career, this book will perhaps nudge him into that direction. To quote renowned investor Peter Lynch: 'Stock market really isn't a gamble, as long as you pick good companies that you think will do well, and not just because of the stock price.'

A word on the organization of the book. It has thirteen chapters. The first chapter highlights popular analogies between the animal and the financial worlds. Each of the next nine chapters focuses on unexplored and exciting animal hunting strategies and behavioural patterns. These strategies are laid down in finer details while drawing similarities to the equity world as well as wider linkages to human behaviour, the business world and the country's development. These analogies are engaging and fun to read. Simultaneously, they are persuasive, motivating readers to derive an understanding of these interrelated worlds and better their investment decisions. These investment themes are explained through relevant examples. Each example portrays the essential things to focus on while deciding to invest, highlighting on what matters, while cutting the noise. The eleventh chapter enumerates the mistakes and the value traps in investing. The twelfth chapter talks about my investment principles, which draw on learnings from philosophy and psychology. The final chapter highlights why we should analyse the S&P 500 index to understand where the BSE Sensex is going.

Equity investing is at least as much an art as it is a science. Bullish and bearish views coexist, and an investor has to pick one before making an investment decision. The Necker cube shown in Figure 1 is the best example to explain shifting perspectives of equity investing.

Figure 1: Necker Cube

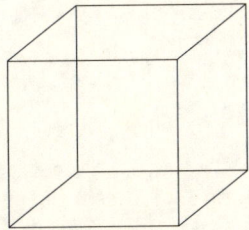

Source: First published in 1832 as a rhomboid by Swiss crystallographer Louis Albert Necker.

· It is a two-dimensional pattern with no particular orientation. Stare at it for a few seconds. At first, it will appear to be a three-dimensional transparent cube facing a specific direction. Keep staring at it, and it will suddenly change to face an opposite direction, only to revert to its original direction when you continue to look at it. The opposite facing transparent cubes are equally compatible with the two-dimensional data on the retina, so our brain effortlessly switches between them. The two opposite directions of the cubes are the bearish and bullish views of any investment. Both coexist at any moment and make equity investing risky and challenging. American publisher and author William Feather said, 'One of the funny things about the market is that every time one person buys, another sells and both think they are astute.' Thus, no book can provide a definite formula for investment success. This book is no exception, and it simply aims to instil thinking that can help one make the right decisions.

Lastly, I have refined my own understanding by writing about these investment themes and organizing them. If at least one soul finds the book useful, I would consider my job well done.

1

THE BEAR CAME FIRST

A DJ draws a connection between two seemingly disparate things and says, 'Look, they are alike. You can dance to them.'

—Kevin Young, American poet

For centuries, the investment world has been riddled with animal references. Many of the investing nomenclatures come from the animal world. The earliest of them is the 'bear'. The name owes its origin to the seventeenth-century practice of traders selling a bear's skin even before having killed the bear. The traders were called 'bearskin jobbers', and by the early 1700s the investors who were short sellers (people who sold stocks they don't own) in the London stock market were being referred to as bearskin jobbers. Their name was quickly shortened to 'bear', and the term has been in vogue ever since. Once the bear found its place in the investing dictionary, the term 'bull' followed. In the Elizabethan era, in the late 1500s, 'bull baiting' and 'bear baiting' were popular and brutal sports like those played in a coliseum. Bull baiting was an alternative to bear baiting and was perhaps considered its opposite.

Possibly, investors who knew their Elizabethan history decided that the opposite of a 'bear' investor was a 'bull' investor who bought stocks in anticipation for it to go higher. Soon usage of the terms bear and the bull became commonplace. In 1720, during the South Sea bubble bust, when the South Sea Company of England failed disastrously, Alexander Pope wrote, 'Come fill the South Sea goblet full; the gods shall of our stock take care: Europa pleased accepts the bull, and Jove with joy puts off the bear'.

I guess this marked the tradition of simplifying investment terminology by borrowing concepts from animal life. Then began the journey of numerous and mysterious connections worth our amusement and inspiration. To continue categorizing investors beyond the bull and bear, the market derived its inspiration from a variety of animals such as pigs, sheep, ostriches, stags and wolves. 'Pigs' refer to greedy and impatient investors, embracing high risks and investing in hot tips to make a quick buck. As the saying goes, 'Bulls make money, bears make money, pigs get slaughtered.'

Similarly, 'sheep' refer to investors without a strategy. If you read this book carefully enough, I bet that you will be anything but a sheep. Another naïve investor category is an 'ostrich', referring to investors who ignore critical and especially, bad news. This is akin to the behaviour of ostriches who bury their heads in the sand upon sensing danger. Then you have 'stags', which imply investors who have nothing to do with bulls or bears. Stags are investors who subscribe to the company's initial public offering (IPO), and sell the shares immediately on listing, hoping to make a quick buck. Lastly, you have the cunning 'wolves'. These are investors who manipulate and scam the market. Often, wolves work in coalition, using 'hunting' techniques to push a company's stock into the ground by shorting the stock.

Animal analogies extend to companies as well. For instance, companies with businesses generating cash consistently are commonly called 'cash cow'. Further, it is common to see a company's high net profit margin (honey), getting eroded with the onset of competition ('honey bee') or high net profit getting eaten away by pushing costs higher 'inflation tapeworm'.

Fortunately, this sort of fun with animal vocabulary does not end here. It penetrates deeper into key corporate and investment concepts. Ever wondered where the term 'diluted' comes from while referring to companies' earnings per share? It comes from livestock traders who would feed their sheep with salt before taking them to the market to sell them by their weight. Salt makes sheep drink a significant amount of water and gain weight. The trader thus dilutes his livestock by increasing the weight, while keeping the amount of meat the same. Investors borrowed the term 'diluted' and appropriately applied it to companies' earnings per share, as in when they are watered down or diluted by issuing new equity shares, while the total net profit remains the same.

In 1807, William Cobbett referred to the term 'red herring' in the *Weekly Political Register*. He said he once used a smoked *red* herring fish (the smoking process turns the herring fish *red* which gives out a strong and pungent smell) to lay a false trail while training hunting dogs. The strong smell of the red herring kept the dogs on a false trail and diverted them from chasing the hare. William used the red herring story as a metaphor to criticize the English press (dogs) of the time because their attention had been intentionally diverted from important domestic matters (hare) by keeping them busy with the false information about a supposed defeat of Napoleon (red herring smell). Gradually, 'red herring' entered investors' parlance. 'Red herring' is now used to describe the draft prospectus, which a company files with the requisite stock exchange authority for approval, ahead of an IPO of debt or equity securities. The draft prospectus is shared with the prospective investors with a prominent disclosure printed in red that the company is not attempting to sell its securities prior to the requisite approvals. It excludes key details such as price and the number of shares offered. Once approvals are received, the prospectus becomes final.

HOW TO BE A SUCCESSFUL INVESTOR

In the Hindi movie *Andhadhun* (2018), the protagonist was a pianist played by Ayushmann Khurrana who temporarily turned himself blind to improve his focus and find inspiration. So much so, that he heard music in every sound. Extreme efforts bring extreme rewards. Similarly, investors can hone their traits by observing a few animals.

Be selective and decisive as a hawk: Hawks can see clearly about eight times as far as an average human, allowing them to spot and focus on a rabbit or any other animal from a distance of about two miles. The hawk is selective and decisive.[1] As the hawk descends from the sky to attack its prey, the muscles in its eyes continuously adjust the curvature of the eyeballs to maintain their piercing focus and a precise perception throughout the approach and attack. Chickens, on the other hand, opt for a buffet-style approach when it comes to feeding. They will eat anything—fruit, vegetables, insects, bugs, fishes, meat and even other chickens. Warren Buffett once said, 'An investor should act as though he had a lifetime decision card with just twenty punches on it.' By this rule, you should think carefully before making any financial decision, and once you are convinced about an investment, your conviction will provide enough confidence to bet a significant portion of your portfolio in that investment. Taking a few investment decisions requires deep research and insight into every investment that you make. It also requires raising the bar and just not accepting any other thing that comes your way. Many renowned investors do not buy a stock unless they believe that it can double in three years. This raised bar compels them to say 'No' most of the time. Before buying your next stock, remember that you are potentially opening the door to losses, mediocre returns and frequent churning of your portfolio. When you care enough to look harder, you can achieve much better returns. You need one right investment to make it big. It is undoubtedly true for Radhakishan Damani with his Avenue Supermarkets (DMART) investment or Rakesh Jhunjhunwala with his investment in Titan Company (TITAN).

Be fearless as a honey badger: Listed as the 'world's most fearless animal' in the Guinness Book of World Records, the honey badger has a long body, which is distinctly thick and broad across the back. Lions, leopards and hyenas are predators who can attempt to kill honey badgers. However, more often than not, these attempts are unsuccessful, as a honey badger will fight incessantly until it is dead or the attacker tires out, at which point the honey badger will escape. After the bankruptcy of Lehman Brothers in September 2008, Warren Buffett in October 2018 displayed the honey badger's fearless qualities by buying US equities when the whole world was falling apart with no hope for better days. In his words, 'The financial world is a mess, both in the United States and abroad. Its problems, moreover, have been leaking into the general economy, and the leaks are now turning into a gusher. In the near term, unemployment will rise, business activity will falter, and headlines will continue to be scary. So...I've been buying American stocks.' He further added, 'A simple rule dictates my buying: Be fearful when others are greedy, and be greedy when others are fearful.'

Carve out a niche like a hummingbird: A hummingbird's extraordinary feat is that it can hover in a place as well as fly backwards, sideways, straight up—with speed. Unlike other birds whose manoeuvrability is restricted to up and down movements. Seeing hummingbirds fly is like magic in the air, especially when they suddenly change direction backwards or sideways. Hummingbirds can rotate their wings, and that allows these acrobatic movements. Businesses and investors should learn to carve out a niche like these elite athletes of the animal world.

Be fox by nature, but a hedgehog by your convictions: Isaiah Berlin in his essay 'The Hedgehog and the Fox' quotes the Greek poet Archilochus's (c. 680-645 BCE), 'The fox knows many things, but the hedgehog knows one big thing.' Foxes pursue many ends, often unrelated and even contradictory. Hedgehogs, however, relate everything to a single vision which in turn defines them. Foxes are nimble and can employ twists and turns to reach their goal. Hedgehogs believe in flattening every obstruction. Foxes and hedgehogs are on two ends of the spectrum—as an investor, try to be in between them and not fixed at either end. Hedgehogs are passive investors, macro believers and investors with concentrated portfolios. Whereas foxes are active investors, investors with diversified portfolios, and their philosophy is unclear and changes frequently. Investors should be foxlike by nature, but hedgehogs by their convictions, that is, they must employ macro trends to actively invest in a diversified portfolio. Hedgehog investors may be prone to psychological denial—as they stick to their big ideas. Fox investors on the other hand, are nimble enough to adjust to the reality. However, the side effect of being a foxlike investor is that they may never hold a stock for a decade, which compounds return consistently. To put it differently, a fox investor will have a bell curve return with higher kurtosis, as they will sacrifice the upside to protect the downside. For hedgehogs, the opposite is true. Hedgehogs will have highly volatile returns due to thicker tails as they leave both the upside and downside open. Most successful investors are both foxes and hedgehogs, as the situation demands. Rakesh Jhunjhunwala, for instance, is a trader—making him a fox—

but he also held his largest portfolio position in Titan Company for a good part of two decades—which makes him a hedgehog concurrently.

Hunt as frogs do: Frogs eat small insects and animals. A frog sits still and waits for its prey to come close to it. Once the prey is within its range, it shoots out its sticky tongue to instantly capture it. Similarly, value investors rarely chase stocks. They wait for the price of their favourite stocks to come within their buying range. Once the opportunity arises, investors waste no time and execute their plans. Hunting tactics of frogs help them save energy as well as increase accuracy. The patience of value investors makes them buy things cheap, while exercising decisiveness.

Fish in a busy pond: The expected return from any investment is a function of the expected return and probability of the same. A lottery ticket can lead to extremely high returns, but the probability is so minute that you would need a microscope to see it. At the other extreme, the probability of expected returns from an AAA-rated sovereign treasury bond in local currency can be close to 100 per cent, but the returns are minuscule. Returns from equity markets and the probability of these returns are somewhere in between. One way to increase this probability is by focusing on the geography and in sectors where the most attractive investments are available. This usually happens when there are macroeconomic and sectoral tailwinds. This increases the expected return. Intuitively 'fishing where most of the fishes are' is always an optimal strategy.

Be an aggressive zebra, when conditions are safe: Ralph Wanger in his book *A Zebra in Lion Country* wrote that equity investors are like zebras in a herd. The key question for any zebra is where to stand in relation to the herd. Outside of the herd is the best, for the grass is fresh there, while those in the middle see only grass which is half-eaten or trampled down. The aggressive zebras, on the outside of the herd, eat much better. On the other hand—or other hoof—there comes a time when lions approach. The outside zebras can end up as a lion's lunch, and the skinny zebras in the middle of the pack may eat less well but they survive. Equity investors are like the grazing herd of zebras. The herd comprises institutional portfolio managers and long-term investors. They both look for above-average return performance and dislike risks, and in zebra parlance, they seek fresh grass. Like zebras being killed by lions, portfolio managers can get fired and long-term investors can lose the investment. A portfolio manager for an institution such as a bank's wealth management department cannot afford to be an *outside zebra*. For him, the optimal strategy is simple: stay in the centre of the herd at all times. As long as he continues to buy the popular stocks he cannot be faulted. To quote one portfolio manager, 'It really doesn't matter a lot to me what happens to Johnson & Johnson as long as everyone has it and we all go down together.' Misery loves company. But on the other hand, a portfolio manager cannot afford to try for large gains on unfamiliar stocks which would leave him open to criticism if the idea fails. For a long-term investor, it pays to be an outside zebra, but actively watch out for lions!

Be ready: Warren Buffett said, 'If you want to shoot rare, fast-moving elephants, you should always carry a loaded gun.' Here Buffett is emphasizing the importance of keeping some portion of the portfolio in cash, to take advantage of temporary dislocations in the market. Without free cash to invest, the investor would be able to enjoy the sight of a rare elephant but they will not be able to monetarily benefit from the sight.

TO ACT OR NOT TO ACT, THAT IS THE QUESTION

For investors, inaction is as important as action. There are many animal proverbs and sayings which try to impart wisdom to investors so they can tell when to act or not. In the case of a boiling frog, Mark Twain's burnt cat and canaries in the coal mine—action is possibly the best strategy.

A 'boiling frog' fable shows that if a frog is suddenly put into boiling water, it will jump out. However, if the same frog is put into warm water, it will not jump out. Then, if the temperature of the water is gradually raised to a boiling point, it will not be able to perceive the danger until the last moment and will be boiled to death. This fable highlights our inability or unwillingness to notice or react to impending threats. This applies to investors' stock positions that continue to bleed. Investors will refrain from exiting the stock and continue to come out with novel reasons to justify their hold. The best strategy in most of such cases is to cut their losses or buy more at lower prices, if convinced—in either case, *take action*. Other examples of 'boiling frogs' are investors sticking to bad investment philosophies and practices, corporates sticking to bad culture and strategies, and individuals sticking to bad personal habits and situations. Some practices and strategies may not be bad, but if they are not in harmony with current macro trends, they can also boil investors and corporates. If they are not corrected by taking appropriate and timely action, then a tipping or boiling point is eventually reached, that is, a point of no return.

Almost one out of ten listed Indian companies lost more than 80 per cent of their value between January 2014 and mid-2019. Investors who had remained inactive were essentially boiled to death. For an investor's portfolio, it becomes even more troubling if these stocks form a significant part of the portfolio. A concentrated portfolio can elevate and also decimate an investor's wealth.

The most notable fund manager to fall in this category is Bruce Berkowitz, the founder of Fairholme Funds. He is a proponent of value investing, strong cash flows and concentrated bets. He made his money in the 2000s, dealing in energy stocks. In 2010, Morningstar, the global financial services firm, named Berkowitz the 'Domestic-Stock Fund Manager' of the decade. In 2011, his asset under management (AUM) peaked at US$ 20. By 2017, it fell to US$ 2.2 billion. The trouble started from 2011 onwards, as he remained devoted to his value investing principle which made him avoid the technology sector. Since 2010, value investing has not been rewarding and most of the index gains have come from the technology sector. His fund was the second largest shareholder of Sears Holdings Corporation (SHLD). SHLD operates a big box retail chain in the US and constituted a significant percentage of Bruce's fund portfolio. SHLD lost 99 per cent of its value since 2010. Bruce's bet was that SHLD's asset sales justified the price he was paying. However, the widening operational losses took him by surprise and reduced the value of the stock significantly. All these years, Bruce remained in denial, as he ignored the macro trend of rising online retailing. In essence, Bruce was boiled as he could not change his investment practice and strategy with the changing times.

In general, mindfulness and frequently evaluating your portfolio and personal life from scratch can be a viable solution against being boiled to death over time. Conversely, good practices if maintained over a long period can create a huge positive difference in your personal life and add a competitive advantage in your professional life. The following equation shows how being boiled at 1 per cent rate every day or putting in 1 per cent of good practice every day for a year makes a big difference:

Status quo: 1 per cent boiled (bad practice) every day for one year.
$$(1-1\%)^{365} = 00.03$$
Take action: 1 per cent good practice every day for one year.
$$(1 + 1\%)^{365} = 37.78$$

To summarize, 1 per cent boiled every day almost finishes you in a year without you noticing it. To the contrary, 1 per cent good practices every day compounds to around thirty-eight times better than your starting point.

Mark Twain once observed, 'If a cat sits on a hot stove, that cat won't sit on a hot stove again. That cat won't sit on a cold stove either. That cat just doesn't like stoves.' The idea of Mark Twain's burnt cat is prevalent in the histories of most investors. It has resulted in investors immediately rejecting many sectors and companies due to their past underperformance or chequered history—creating opportunities for value investors and contrarian bets, especially when the future is expected to be significantly brighter than the past. Instead of shunning it, the taking of measured action is the need of the hour. At the macro level, Mark Twain's burnt cat results in multiyear/decade secular bull and bear phases in the stock market.

In a secular bull phase, the index reaches new highs frequently. In a secular bear phase, the index trades below its last all-time highs for years and decades. Once the multiyear/decade all-time high levels are breached, then the index starts a new bull phase. To explain this further, let us consider the S&P 500, one of the oldest and most mature equity market indexes available globally. The index has experienced two secular bull phases since the 1950s. The first secular bull phase continued from 1954 to 1973 and was halted by approximately 48 per cent market corrections from January 1973 to October 1974. The index then continued to trade below its January 1973 peak until 1982. In 1982, the previous peak was breached, and the secular bull phase started, which continued from 1982 to 2000. It was halted by about 49 per cent market corrections from March 2000 and October 2002. The index continued to trade below March 2000 levels, and from October 2007 to March 2009, the index again fell by approximately 55 per cent. In 2013, the S&P 500 breached the March 2000 peak, and started its new secular bull phase. During these bull phases, an index does see corrections, but they are relatively shallow (up to 37 per cent historically), and these corrections are recuperated within a year or two while the index goes on to make new highs. This is unlike in a bear secular phase where close to 50 per cent of correction is common and recouping the fall takes many years.

Do note that the past two secular bull phases were seventeen and eighteen years long. The bull phase lasts this long because this period is needed for most of the experienced and burnt investors (who refuse to sit on a hot stove again) to exit the market, and for the newcomers who have never experienced a hot stove to continue the secular bull phase until it meets its end. As the saying goes—there is no old and bold investor.

A canary in a coal mine alerts us as to when we should spring into action. For a long time since 1911, miners in Great Britain had started the tradition of carrying a caged canary bird down into the mines. In the mines, odourless carbon monoxide can build up to deadly levels. These gaseous build-ups negatively affect canaries much earlier than when they become harmful for humans. Thus, when the canary weakened or stopped singing, it would sound as an alarm bell for the miners to get out of the mines immediately. In 1986, electronic warning devices replaced these birds. Nevertheless, in the financial coal mine, the canary continues to provide an early warning signal of the oncoming grave dangers to the investors and signals the time for them to throw in the towel.

Starting in the third week of July 2007, credit default spreads started to widen in the West from historically low levels. Well, if this seemed too early to ring a warning alarm, then in March 2008, the investment bank, Bear Sterns, fell prey to a liquidity crisis as subprime mortgage defaults accelerated in the US. Bear Sterns was the canary. What followed was the worst financial crisis since 1929. If investors had taken note of the Bear Stern canary, they would have escaped a lot of misery and financial loss.

This is just one of the many examples of what happens when one bank's failure signals a deteriorating liquidity landscape and trouble for the entire banking sector. The other examples of canaries in the corporate world are:

- Mass sell-off of speculative small capitalization stocks which signal any oncoming risk-off attitude and trouble for the whole market.
- A sector-wide rise in capital expenditure which signals an oncoming excess capacity, leverage problems, lower capacity utilization and weak earnings due to operational deleveraging.
- Rising regulatory watch on a sector calls for oncoming sector-wide trouble (for example, healthcare, banks) irrespective of how well a constituent company is managed.
- Sector-wide hype calls for sharp sell-offs shortly (technology stocks in 1999/2000; infrastructure and real state stocks in 2007; Indian non-banking financial companies [NBFC] stocks in 2017).

- Bad monsoons signal trouble for agriculture and rural-driven consumer businesses.
- Sector leaders reporting significantly below than expected quarterly financials, signals bad times for the sector and all its constituent companies.
- The 2018 Infrastructure Leasing and Financial Services (IL&FS) default was the canary in India's financial services mine.

One's fearful disposition often senses canaries that are only present in one's minds. To avoid unjustified bearishness, the rule of thumb to sense imminent danger is the presence of canaries as well as existing vulnerability. Both together ring an alarm bell, while alone they are just unfounded fears.

Canaries + Vulnerability = Danger Ahead

To substantiate further, if you look at the US and the global economies, then there have been multiple canaries post the 2009's great financial crisis:

- 2011: MF Global collapse
- 2012: Europe's recession
- 2013: US Federal Reserve taper tantrum (fear of a rise in the interest rates due to lower bond purchases by the US Federal Reserve)
- Late 2015 to early 2016: China hard landing fears (sharp GDP growth slowdown below 4 per cent)
- Early 2016: Commodity price collapse
- 2016: Brexit
- Late 2016: Donald Trump's election
- 2018: EM liquidity crisis, especially in Turkey and Argentina
- Late 2018: US equity bear market

The US and the global economies have continued to muddle through somehow. The real canary that can push these economies into their next recession is a rising inflation (consistently above 2.5 per cent) in the US. Until that occurs, a low inflation would mean that the US Federal Reserve can continue to supply global financial coal mines with fresh air (that is, keep interest rates low), thereby diluting the carbon monoxide (that is, risks), and keeping the miners (that is, investors) safe.

Let us move from when investors should act to when they shouldn't act. Inaction is best for investors when faced with 'Warren Buffett's horse'. Warren Buffett once quoted Samuel Johnson, 'A horse that can count to ten is a remarkable horse, not a remarkable mathematician.' Warren Buffett was hinting at how you should not be betting on industries with unattractive economics due to significant headwinds, competition or other challenges. This is irrespective of how good a company's management appears. Even a first class management would not be able to do much under such circumstances. Warren Buffett himself is an apt example—he was not able to improve the original textile business of Berkshire Hathaway due to inferior industry economics and closed it down (preferred inaction).

Again, inaction can be a good strategy when investors are behaving like a Pavlovian dog. Ivan Pavlov conducted an experiment in which he would ring a bell to feed a dog. Then, after repeating this procedure, he rang the bell without providing food to the dog. The sound of the bell made the dog salivate even when there was no food. The dog learnt to associate the ringing of the bell with food. Similarly, investors often naively associate great returns from investments to macro or sector level factors, and discount the subtle role that micro and company level factors are playing. It is of no wonder that during the technology boom many companies with dot com names were floated to benefit from investors' faulty associations. Similarly, the rise of Bitcoin gave birth to so many other cryptocurrencies. In India, when Lovable Lingerie (LOVABLE) went public, investors flocked to it thinking it would be the next Page Industry (PAGEIND, owner of the Jockey brand). Investors failed to realize that Page Industry's success is due to various factors unique to itself, and is not due to undergarment sector tailwind. Similarly, an early success in a particular strategy or a certain type of investment attracts significantly higher capital flows later on. Moreover, most of the time, the early success is due to some secondary reinforcement, which gradually disappears.

Antidotes to avoid being pawned by past or early success are to:

- judiciously scrutinize past success, look for a chance; non-causative factors associated with past successes as they tend to mislead as you appraise a related proposed new investment; and
- scrutinize past success for risky features appearing in the new investment, ones that were absent when the past success occurred.

ANIMAL SPIRITS MEET BLACK SWAN

The movie *Wall Street* is a must watch for every MBA student, and I saw it around that time in my life. The protagonist Gordon Gekko's insightful speech still remains fresh. He said, 'Greed, for lack of a better word, is good. Greed is right, greed works. Greed clarifies, cuts through and captures the essence of the evolutionary spirit. Greed, in all of its forms; greed for life, for money, for love, knowledge has marked the upward surge of mankind.'

'Animal spirits' is a term coined by John Maynard Keynes to describe instincts, proclivities and emotions that allegedly influence and guide human behaviour. Greed for money and progress is the 'animal spirit' that drives entrepreneurs and risk-takers who rarely have the luxury to do a precise quantitative analysis before venturing into uncharted territory. They are driven by their gut feeling or intuition, or just simple greed. First-mover disadvantage is high, but they march along with their vision as their only guiding torch. If it were not for them, societies would have remained agrarian and in rural settings. Entrepreneurs' animal spirits is a necessary evil. It leads to excesses though. Eventually, when greed grips firmly, then the unstoppable economic momentum is halted by an unpredictable or unforeseen crisis aka 'Black Swan'. The term was popularized by Nassim Nicholas Taleb in his book *The Black Swan*.

Animal spirits eventually meets a black swan—a crisis; however, the price is worth the progress. As the price paid is temporary, the progress is permanent and provides crucial steps for further progress. The closest example for me is Dubai. In the last twenty years, Dubai has become a modern city with a brand new infrastructure—much better than the established developed world. When the government embarked on this journey of development in the late 1990s, all it had was a large barren land and a vision. Not oil, which sits with its neighbour, Abu Dhabi, the capital city. Dubai relied on the prophecy, 'Build it and they will come.' In the last twenty years, they have seen it all: go-go years; the brink of bankruptcy and stability. Finally, it's now a modern city which attracts people from all parts of the world, and all this started with nothing but arid land.

Animals have traversed the earth before us and have been co-existing with us. Thus, they have become an essential part of many subjects that are close to human beings. Humans knowingly, or unknowingly, have learned various aspects of investing from them and this book is an attempt to further that learning.

2

LION'S OPPORTUNITY—CAN CATCH THEM ALL

We don't have a monopoly. We have market share. There's a difference.

—Steve Ballmer, ex-CEO, Microsoft

Looking for greener pastures, roughly 1.5 million[1] wildebeest migrate from the Serengeti National Park in Tanzania to the Masai Mara National Reserve in Kenya from July to October. Wildebeest or the 'wild beast' has been named for its frighteningly large head, shaggy lock, pointed beard and curved horns. Along with wildebeest, roughly 0.8 million zebras and gazelles form the migration herd. This journey of approximately 2.3 million herbivorous animals has no real beginning or end. Whether in Kenya or Tanzania, they are constantly on the move. The wildebeest's life is an endless search for grass and water.

In comparison to the herbivores, the number of carnivorous predators (lions, cheetahs and hyenas) is far fewer and contained. Recent estimates put less than 1,000 lions[2] and very few cheetahs in Masai Mara. Food is the farthest concern for these predators. The wildebeest normally weighs between 350 to 550 pounds,[3] and becomes an easy and dependable source of food for the predators. A lion can eat up to fifteen wildebeests during the migration period. Hence, Masai Mara's lions altogether eat a maximum of 15,000 wildebeests during these four months. This number is roughly at 1 per cent of the 1.5 million migrating wildebeests. Besides, the analysis ignores lions who hunt zebras and gazelles. To put it simply, the opportunity or market size for the lions is just too big. They are spoiled for choice and can usually choose the weakest of the herd. Moreover, with so much food around, there is no competition from other predators—the cheetahs and the hyenas.

For the wildebeests, predation is not the only peril. They have to guard themselves against injury and exhaustion as well. Together, these perils kill over 0.25 million[4] wildebeests every year. Nevertheless, up to 0.5 million[5] calves are born during February and March every year, ensuring that the market size for the lions is restocked.

THE WORLD IS OUR PLAYGROUND

Albert Einstein is widely credited with a saying that compound interest 'is the most powerful force in the universe'. A company can unleash this power by compounding its net worth (equity capital) for a very long period at a healthy return on equity (that is, higher than the cost of equity). To be able to do that, the corporation has to be the lion of the corporate world. Corporates become lions when they have a competitive advantage that allows them to exploit a large market size and squeeze out the competition, if any. While such a competitive advantage ensures a high return on equity (RoE) it is not enough. Besides, a large and growing market is enough to ensure a long runway to allow their compounding power to be unleashed. Remarkably, a lion of the wild has all of the above:

- a competitive advantage in the form of its claws;
- a large market size of 1.5 million wildebeests; and
- a growing market as wildebeests breed rapidly.

Corporates that are leaders or dominant in their markets can be placed into four different quadrants as given in Table 2.1. Each quadrant contains non-exhaustive examples of leaders in that quadrant:

Table 2.1: Ownership and Target Market Matrix

	Niche market	Mass market
Private-controlled	Indian Energy Exchange Zydus Wellness	**Lions!** <u>Amazon</u> <u>Google</u> <u>Uber</u> <u>Visa</u> Bajaj Finance <u>Facebook</u> Maruti Suzuki HDFC Bank Nestle India Dmart
Government-controlled	Cochin Shipyard Mishra Dhatu Nigam	State Bank of India Coal India

Note: The companies that are not underlined are Indian companies.
Source: Author.

There are many leaders. A unique competitive advantage generally makes for a corporate leader and increases its market share over a period of time. However, lions are few in number. A large market size makes a leader, a lion. A large market size allows for the compounding of the net worth over a long period. For global corporates like Amazon, Google, Facebook, Uber, Visa and others, the global population of more than 7.5 billion[6] is the actual market size. Addressing such a large market size brings its challenges, as well as competition into play. These companies have reached a pole position and can rightfully be called the 'lions of the global corporate world'. Then there are the Indian corporates like Bajaj

Finance, DMART, Nestle India, HDFC Bank that have 1.3 billion[7] Indians as their market size. They too can be rightfully called the 'lions of the Indian corporate world'. If we were to look at it from another perspective, all these corporations are also like whales in an ocean. On the contrary, a leader in a niche market is but a big fish in a small pond. Irrespective of the size of the fish, the runway (size of the pool) is limited and the niche market player will eventually hit a dead end. This does not mean that a niche leader cannot be attractive. They definitely can be, but not for a very long-term buy and hold strategy; in such a scenario, a leader in a mass market would do a better job. Besides, the leaders of mass markets are bigger companies and should be preferred, as they have crossed many critical milestones.

Control is key while distinguishing a lion from a leader. Lions are privately controlled corporations, and rarely are they controlled by a government. A privately controlled corporation is more enterprising and keeps the company ahead of the competition. A government-controlled entity can also beat competition consistently. However, that happens when they have privileged access to critical resources, or regulatory support or an access to cheap financing; not because of an enterprising spirit that is critical for survival. Furthermore, due to their wider interests and obligations, a government company often would have mandates that hurt rather than enhance the shareholder returns.

LION'S CLAWS

The claws of a wild lion put it at the top of the food chain. Its claws are almost 1.5 inches long, and are very sharp in order to quickly knock its prey out. Similarly, corporate lions have their own invincible claws, that is, their competitive advantage. The sources of these advantages are varied, but they all promise unmatched value and convenience to their customers. Amazon's claws are the low prices it offers to its customers on a wide variety of products. Amazon also provides conveniences when it comes to shopping as well as a same-day delivery option. For Facebook and Visa, their 'network effect' acts as their claws. The network effect is the phenomenon where the value of a product is enhanced when more and more people use it. Similar to a telephone or an email account, Facebook is of no use if it is available to only one user. The usability of Visa's payment card increases significantly with the rising number of users as it prompts more and more merchants and vendors to accept the Visa card. The same is true for electric cars. The increase in usage of electric cars in a city will accelerate the installation of charging points across the city, and further accelerate the usage of electric cars. The opposite of this network effect is the notion of exclusivity which applies to electricity. Say, if you were the only exclusive one to have electricity in your home, then its value would be immense.

Coming to some of the Indian lions, Dmart or Avenue Supermarts (DMART) derives its claws by providing grocery products at competitive prices. Bajaj Finance (BAJFINANCE) has built a diversified retail lending behemoth by leveraging data analytics to cross-sell a suite of lending products to an existing customer base. Nestle India benefits immensely from its brand value, which ensures customer loyalty. Maruti Suzuki benefits from competitive pricing as well as the network effect of an ecosystem consisting of distribution channels and after sale service stations.

Quantitative proof of these corporate lions' claws is that they have consistently generated double-digit revenue growth, barring a few exceptional years; they have earned at least mid to high teens in return on equity; have hardly had any debt and rather, have significant cash sitting on their balance sheet.

CONTAINED NICHE LEADERS

A niche market leader initially grows fast in its specialized category. With time, as it garners a significant market share, it starts to face growth challenges. Further market share gains become challenging, and the niche leader has to rely on an overall market growth. At this point, maintaining a profit margin can also become challenging for the leader, as weaker competitors start to compete for survival—resulting in cut-throat competition. The niche leader, like a fox, is running for the market share, that is, food, while its weaker competitor, like a rabbit, runs for survival. A tough fight must ensue.

Indian markets have some interesting examples of niche leaders. The Indian Energy Exchange (IEX) and Multi Commodity Exchange of India (MCX) are prominent Indian exchanges for power and commodity trading, respectively. These exchange houses have garnered more than 90 per cent of the market share in their respective categories. Exchanges receive preferential attachment due to the network effect of a rising user base, providing liquidity and facilitating market efficiency. Another company with a 90 per cent plus market share is Zydus Wellness (ZYDUSWELL). Its precise market share is 94.2 per cent 2018,[8] making it almost a monopoly when it comes to sugar substitute products. Despite the high market share, its total revenue from the Sugar Free products is less than Rs 350 crore. Nonetheless, its Sugar Free product is highly profitable (20 per cent plus net margin)[9] and the money that has been generated from the product has helped the company diversify, mostly through inorganic acquisitions, into other categories such as malted drinks, talcum powder, clarified butter, skincare cosmetics and butter alternatives. Due to the diversification, Sugar Free's contribution to the revenue is now roughly 20 per cent,[10] a far cry from its historic 75 per cent plus contribution. Zydus Wellness is a poster boy of a big fish's transition from a small pond to an ocean.

3

KORI BUSTARD'S FEATHER—TRIGGER FOR INVESTMENT ACTION

Next in importance to having a good aim is to recognize when to pull the trigger.

—David Letterman, American television host

Throughout most of Sub-Saharan Africa, the kori bustards are frequently seen flying low, ambushing and opportunistically trailing close to huge animals such as elephants or buffaloes. As the large animals move through longer grasses and uproot ground-dwelling insects, the kori bustard suddenly flies down, snatching the insects.

In a different setting, a similar aerial form of hunting takes place on the back of Africa's heaviest flying bird the kori bustard. The kori bustard tolerates small birds such as the southern carmine bee-eater, perching on its back. The southern carmine bee-eaters, also known as 'tick-birds', pluck ticks and ectoparasites off the skin of the animals they are roosting on. The carmine riding on the kori bustard uses the bustard as a perch to catch flying insects flushed out by the kori bustard's feathers. After the kill, the carmine resumes its position only to repeat the process again. Rarely are relationships in the animal kingdom this harmonic. Other small birds such as the northern carmine, cattle egret, wattled starlings and black fork-tailed drongos also associate themselves similarly with large moving animals and grazers.[1] By staying close to the source, these birds behave opportunistically. This strategy allows them to prey on many insects while reducing their time or effort, as opposed to chasing insects, one by one.

What is interesting about this strategy is that it is effective and quick. By being close to the reoccurring and embedded trigger, that is, grazing large animals, or the kori bustard's feathers consistently flushing insects—birds make sure that there is a consistent supply of insects to catch and prey on. The need to feed on many insects made a few birds devise a strategy of staying close to the source that uproots or flushes insects. Perhaps, those smart birds (and their followers) procreated better and passed on this trait through generations and eventually all birds started to practise this strategy.

A BUFFET OF SALMON FOR BEARS

Salmon are freshwater fish that migrate down into the ocean to grow. After they have matured, they return to upstream to spawn. The return journey requires salmon to run up the rivers and leap up the waterfalls—a risky affair. During the months of July and August, brown bears flock to Brooks Falls in the Katmai National Park and Preserve to take full advantage of this phenomenon. Bears stand at the edge of the waterfall with their mouths open. From a few feet down below, many salmon would leap up in the air to jump over the waterfalls. It is a delightful scene. Some would end up in the bears' mouths. Nevertheless, many escape and safely land in the water. Salmon continue their run up until they reach the place of their birth. It is estimated that in a day, a bear can catch as many as 25 to 35 salmon. Very much like kori bustard's feather, the edge of the waterfall provides free lunch to brown grizzly bears.

THE TRIGGER

Triggers are instant and very impactful unlike the gradual change which generates new opportunities.

A trigger is any action that bears the fruit of one's past efforts. In this sense, a trigger follows some gradual change. For example, the examination result of a student, job offers, a sports competition, corporate spin-offs and bonus earnings, among others. Such triggers bring into play a hidden but existing value, thereby separating the chaff from the wheat. Usain Bolt was on the race track for only two minutes. Those two minutes were the trigger that fructified over twenty years of effort and went on to earn him fame and fortune. Tesla Model S received accolades in 2012, but its popularity was triggered when *Motor Trend* magazine, one of the most popular automobile magazines, named the Model S as the car of the year in 2013. Since then, both car sales and share prices have skyrocketed.

Existing Value + Trigger = Excess Returns

Triggers not only fructify past efforts but also enable value creation. Examples of such triggers include weather conditions, election results, reforms and legislations affecting businesses, scientific inventions, authority approvals, corporate actions and so on. These enablers create value rather than simply unlock existing value. Key triggers that pushed civilization to where it is today was the invention of the wheel, the nail, the printing press, gunpowder, electricity, the steam engine, the telephone, vaccinations and the internet!

Ubiquity

Triggers are ubiquitous. From nature to scientific invention, to politics to the business world, triggers are present everywhere. Staying within the focus of this book, let us look at the triggers present in the corporate world. In the corporations, most changes are gradual. Gradual changes are tough to estimate, and even when estimated properly, may take a long time to reflect on the financial status and for the markets to recognize and price it. To the contrary, a trigger is a noticeable change that facilitates a much speedier pricing by the markets. Interestingly, a gradual change meets a tipping point when it reaches a critical mass or upon encountering a trigger that brings the change to the notice of the market.

The triggers we are interested in are those events that immediately influence the company's financials or its market value in a substantial way. The immediate impact is important as it reduces the wait time. Such triggers come from both macro and micro events. Most common macro factors are acts of God, terrorism or government regulations and decisions. Common acts of God are rains, hurricanes, tornadoes and so on. Government regulations can be sector-specific, or they may be something that can potentially affect the entire economy, such as the demonetization decision of the Indian government in November 2016.

Most common micro events arise from corporate actions, such as listing of a subsidiary company (Majesco Limited), selling loss-generating assets (Heritage Foods), management change (Uniply Industries, Safari Industries), receiving critical regulatory approvals (most pharma companies), demergers (Kaya Limited, Intellect Design Arena, Triveni Turbine, Greenply Industries, Transport Corporation of India, Crompton Greaves), share buybacks, open offers, debt restructuring and similar other actions.

Timing is key here. Investors have to be smart enough to decipher the presence, as well as the timing of the trigger. Most outsized gains come from not-so-obvious triggers identified early on before they are apparent to the markets. Nonetheless, I have observed that once the trigger is known, the market takes quite a bit of time to unlock the value produced by the trigger. So even if you are unable to identify a trigger beforehand, even positioning yourself once the trigger is on it can be sufficiently rewarding. A trigger not only reduces the investors' wait time, but also enhances the certainty of unlocking value. Thus it lowers chances of landing into and holding onto a value trap indefinitely. Also, the trigger somewhat protects an investor from the downside, especially in cases where the market has not yet priced in the value that is due to the trigger.

It is crucial to stay close to the trigger—much like staying close to a large animal grazing, or waiting closely for the kori bustard's feathers to flush out helpless insects. But you should also keep in mind that triggers do not always bring opportunities and many times bring casualties (as faced by black money hoarders in 2016 due to demonetization).

KEY GLOBAL MACRO TRIGGERS OF THE LAST DECADE

In December 2008, the US Federal Reserve (Fed) started to print money to buy bonds (quantitative easing) and that resulted in the longest bull market in US history. In mid-2013, the Fed decided to wind down the quantitative easing and that led to the capital market being sold off globally and especially in the emerging markets (including India). Other minor triggers were Narendra Modi's election victory in 2014, demonetization in India in 2016, the Brexit referendum in 2016, Donald Trump's election victory in 2016, China's pollution control drive through the 2016-20 five-year plan (benefitting steel and aluminium prices) among others.

Mohamed Bouazizi

In December 2010, a seemingly trivial incident became a trigger that initiated a chain reaction globally and resulted in vast ramifications. A young Tunisian fruit vendor, Mohamed Bouazizi, did not have the funds to bribe the local police and was humiliated and harassed to the point that he had to give up street vending. Dejected, he set himself on fire and this sparked wide protests in Tunisia, led by other unemployed youth. The demonstrations arose in Oman, Yemen, Egypt, Syria, Libya, Tunisia and Morocco and led to the downfall of the autocratic presidents and leaders of Tunisia, Egypt, Libya and Yemen. Many of them had remained in power for decades much to the dissatisfaction of their citizens. The demonstration is popularly known as the Arab Spring. Its impact was transmitted beyond the Middle East due to the rise of illegal immigration from these countries and through various changes in financial markets. The broad unrest in the region raised fears of the disruption of oil supply from the region and artificially kept oil prices above US$ 100 per barrel until mid-2014, reflecting a high political risk premium. On the other hand, all the other commodities during this period saw a significant fall in prices, marking the end of the super-cycle of commodity prices that had begun in 2002. The artificially high oil prices during the Arab Spring accelerated the US shale oil boom, amplifying the oil supply-demand mismatch. Eventually, the political risk premium subsided, resulting in a sharp decline in oil prices during 2015 and onto early 2016. This led to the steep global market sell-off early that very year. That is, sovereign wealth funds of the oil-exporting countries sold their global financial assets to make up for lower oil revenues and rising budget deficits. The sell-off affected oil producers, consumers, investors, governments, sovereign funds, corporates, individuals among others. The dots can be connected endlessly. I can bet Mohamed Bouazizi affected you in multiple ways!

The above example exhibits the significance of a trigger. An equally important factor is also the presence of all the other ingredients that can support the subsequent effects of the trigger, which may then result in something big. Thus, identifying a trigger is crucial, but one has to monitor its effects in order to foretell and benefit from the outcomes.

To quote from *Does God Play Dice? The New Mathematics of Chaos* by Ian Stewart, 'The flapping of a single butterfly's wing today produces a tiny change in the state of the atmosphere. Over a period of time, what the atmosphere actually does diverges from what it would have done. So, in a month's time, a tornado that would have devastated the Indonesian coast doesn't happen. Or maybe one that wasn't going to happen, does.'

Acts of God: Escorts Ltd.

Acts of God as the name suggests, are inherently unpredictable. If you could predict them with a reasonable degree of certainty, then you would surely have been laughing your way to the bank. I encountered something similar in the end of 2015. In India, between 2003 and 2013, the rainfall deficit had not exceeded 10 per cent for two consecutive years. But in 2014 and 2015, the deficit was 12 per cent[2] plus, a rare occurrence due to El-Nino. Based on the historical data, it was highly likely that in 2016, the monsoon should be favourable. Expectation of a favourable monsoon in 2016 was the 'kori bustard's feather', which would have yielded many insects for me to feed on. I just wanted one extremely nutritious insect to feed on. Therefore, in late 2015, I started hunting for a company which was most leveraged to a favourable monsoon in 2016. Escorts Ltd. was one such company. Escorts manufactures tractors which provides 80 per cent of its revenues, and the remaining 20 per cent comes from the auto ancillary, railways and construction equipment.

From 2011 to 2015, Escorts's revenue and profit deteriorated gradually, mostly due to poor monsoons and dampened tractor sales since 2014. Additionally, Escorts's products were absent in the 41-50 horse power category and haulage tractors. In addition, it made a strategic error by defocusing in states that ultimately ended up growing stronger. It was a perfect cocktail of a lousy macro and micro environment.

Table 3.1: Escorts's Financials

Fiscal Year 2015 (Rs Billion)	Consolidated
Market capitalization	20
Net Debt	2
Enterprise value (EV)	22 (20 + 2)
Revenue	41
EBITDA (Earnings before interest, tax, depreciation and amortization)	1.6
EV/EBITDA	14x

Source: Escorts Limited Annual Reports 2015 (available at https://www.escortsgroup.com/images/annualreport/Annual_Report_2015_16.pdf, accessed on 21 July 2019)

To fix the situation, Escorts resorted to business restructuring since 2014. It lowered its raw material costs, reduced excess workforce and launched six new models to fix gaps in its portfolio. It also strengthened its hold in weaker states. Even then, the market did not recognize the company's efforts as these actions were not reflected in the top or bottom line in a decisive manner due to low-capacity utilization. This did indicate a potential for high operating leverage play, but only once sales returned.

In 2001 and 2002, the tractor industry witnessed a steep contraction. Nevertheless, it came back equally strong. During the years 2004 through 2006, their sales grew almost 20 per cent on average due to the pent-up tractor demand. Thus, the industry's history hints that better times were ahead. Moreover, an ongoing long-term trend of rising usage of farm equipment, to counter rising wages, augurs well for the tractor industry.

Given all the above factors, it was primed for an upward move with the onset of a favourable monsoon. As expected, the monsoon in 2016 was normal, and provided the expected trigger to Escorts. The company saw its tractor sales jump by 20 plus per cent and its earnings before interest, tax, depreciation and amortization (EBITDA) almost doubled in the fiscal year 2017 (the fiscal year in India starts in April and ends in March of the following year). The share price more than kept pace with the company's improving scenario and the market capitalization rose to Rs 77 billion, almost 3.5 times between end 2015 and May 2019.

I realized that predicting the trigger was important. However, it was more important to pick the company which was most leveraged to this trigger, to make the most of this accurate prediction. For instance, Mahindra and Mahindra is the market leader in the tractor industry and derives 20 per cent of its revenue from it; 60 per cent of its revenues comes from automobiles, and it has always been an efficient player in all its businesses. So during this period while Escorts's rose 3.5 times, Mahindra's share prices remained stagnant. Mahindra's share prices remained stagnant as it is already a well-run company and tractors form a small portion of its business.

China's Speeding Ticket

Four decades of rapid Chinese economic growth and exports have done wonders for the country. From strengthening the yuan's value, to making China the largest non-US holder of US treasury bonds, to raising its domestic living standard and making China an economic superpower.

The critical trigger came in 2001 when China joined the WTO. Since then, Chinese exports have skyrocketed. However, this growth is not without hangovers. It has created a significant overcapacity of commodities and heavy industries, leading to commodity price corrections, from 2010/2011 onwards. Further, it has turned China into the world's No 1 carbon dioxide emitter—emitting almost 9 billion tonnes annually. Its carbon emission has been rising for the last four decades, and has tripled since it joined the WTO. Almost two-fifths of its exports went to the US and Europe. While it relieved the West of all the associated pollution, it has resulted in manufacturing job losses and rise of populism in the US and Europe. The Brexit referendum and Trump's victory in 2016 are direct by-products of China's growing manufacturing sector.

China continued to brush the pollution problem under the carpet. Until 2008, the pollution levels were a state secret. However, the Chinese government had to accept the dilemma when it had become rampant from 2013 onwards. According to the Chinese Academy of Social Sciences, pollution-related concerns were behind half of the large-scale protests in China during 2013, making pollution the leading cause of social instability. To address the problem, in late 2013, China introduced environmental policies and regulations that featured concrete and actionable measures to control pollution, as well as specific milestones to be achieved by 2020. In 2014, the government decided to scrap six million old cars, off the road. The mother of all triggers came in October 2015 when the government released a preliminary summary of its 2016-20, five-year plan. The plan laid out aggressive targets to control pollution. It emphasized on reducing coal usage, which meant slashing steel and aluminium outputs as they are primary coal users. The plan also focused on carrying out pollution abatement projects in fifteen key industries, including waste paper, chemicals, plastics and building materials. The government included environmental metrics in the performance assessment of local government officials to ensure effective implementation of the new laws and regulations. Environment regulations and implementation measures were the triggers that were to yield enough insects across sectors, for the investing birds to feed on.

Then came the time of implementation. In 2016, China slashed 45 million tonnes of its steel output, and reduced coal mining operation days from 330 to 276 days.[3] Both coal and steel prices have consequently skyrocketed. In April 2017, the government targeted a reduced production of aluminium by 11 per cent.[4] In November 2017, aluminium smelters and alumina refineries were required to curb output by 30 per cent during[5] the months of November to March to reduce winter smog. Suppliers of carbon products to the smelting sector have had to cut their output by 50 per cent if they met all environmental standards, or unconditionally by 100 per cent if they failed to do so. Consequently, aluminum prices rose significantly during 2016 and 2017, and the US/EU aluminium smelters restarted operations as the Chinese output fell.

Indian companies have benefited immensely. Most of the steel, aluminium, paper and chemical companies saw a stellar rise in their share prices in 2016 and 2017.

Planned Serendipity

Many Indian corporations often own a core business that is mature, but has a low growth potential. Alongside this, they also own a niche-related or unrelated business that provides significant growth potential and return metrics. Such situations, especially concerning the coexistence of two unrelated businesses with different fundamentals, are mostly an outcome of serendipity. Serendipity is tough for investors to predict. More so, there is only a limited benefit for investors when they do predict an occurrence of serendipity under such circumstances. The revenue from core, mature, low-growth business camouflages the revenue from niche fast-growing business. Thus, the fast growth and superior fundamentals of the niche business remains somewhat hidden from the wider stock market participants. Consequently, the company does not enjoy superior valuation, despite having stumbled upon such niche businesses. In such cases, corporate action in the form of spinning-off is undertaken to list the niche business as a separate entity in the bourses. Spin-offs result in value unlocking because the niche entity gains the attention of the stock market. The Indian market annually throws out at least 3 to 4 lucrative spin-off opportunities. These opportunities result in planned serendipity for new investors. Because these investors are investing with full information and the company's serendipity in front of them, but without really paying for it as the market does not value the business fairly.

The key question to ask here is why the market fails to value the niche business fairly. The explanation has to be about more than just the occurrence of camouflage revenue. Perhaps the lack of separate identity raises the market's scepticism around the niche business's ability to function without its parent's support. It may also be attributed to the robustness of the financial metrics. Moreover, a lack of detailed, segmental financial reporting around the niche business's profitability and capital ratios is also a major barrier to the market in prescribing fair value to it. Furthermore, after the spin-off has taken effect, the full details around its financials take a while to appear. Therefore, post-listing, the niche business continues to trade for quite some time at a discount until it starts reporting its quarterly and annual profits and then gradually attracts analyst coverage and the wider interest of investors.

GULF OIL LUBRICANTS (GULFOILLUB)

Gulf Oil Corporation (GOCLCORP), owned by the Hinduja Group, started as an industrial explosives business almost fifty years ago. In 1993, it diversified into a lubricant business which became the second largest player in the retail lubricant market in India. After lubricants, it gradually diversified into mining and infrastructure services, property development, building products and specialty chemicals, etc. But none of the businesses has been able to prove its merit. Progressively after 2009, the lubricant business has generated more profits and cash than the whole group combined. Yes, a clear thumbs down on the management's capital allocation ability. The situation is similar to one where a son's earnings sustain the lavish spending of all the other incapable siblings (which, by the way, is not very uncommon in India's joint family setting).

The prescription given to both the joint family and the business is to separate the large family. In February 2013, the board announced a demerger or spin-off of the lubricant business into a pure play company, one that would be separately listed. Lubricants is a good business from many perspectives. The business buys commodities and sells brands, allowing for consistent price hikes, thereby taking care of the margin. A few players dominate the industry, and they do not compete on retail prices. The emphasis is on branding, marketing, incentivizing dealers to push the product, expanding distribution reach, tying up with original equipment manufacturers (OEMs), as well as consistently introducing innovative, value-added products.

Since 2002, the lubricant business' revenue grew at a compounded annual growth rate of around 30 per cent per annum—from Rs 0.5 billion in the fiscal year 2002, to Rs 9.7 billion in the fiscal year 2013.[6] Growth came partly from capacity expansion and partly from price rises. The lubricant business consistently raised its market shares. Its 30 per cent annual growth was higher than that of its competitors: Castrol grew at 9.5 per cent per annum; Savita Oil Technologies at 20.5 per cent per annum. The lubricant business was generating a return on capital employed of approximately 65 per cent. A huge number remained invisible to the markets due to the management's diversification into unrelated and unattractive businesses.

Table 3.2: Gulf Oil Corporation's Financials

Fiscal Year 2013 (Rs Billion)	Consolidated (FY 2013)	Other Business (FY 2013)	Lubricant Business (FY 2013)
Market capitalization	10	–	–
Net debt	18	–	–
Enterprise value	28 (10 + 18)	–	–
Revenue	13.3	3.6	9.7
Net profit	0.5	– 0.3	0.8
Implied market capitalization	10	0 (no value for loss-making units)	10 (implying 2% growth rate and 10% discount rate)

Source: GOCL Corporation Limited Annual Report 2013 (available at https://www.bseindia.com/stock-share-price/financials/annualreports/506480/, accessed on 22 July 2019)

The market capitalization of GOCLCORP then was close to Rs 10 billion. If we assume zero value for the loss-making of all the other businesses, the market was attributing Rs 10 billion for the lubricant business. Against this, during the fiscal year 2014, the lubricant business was expected to earn a net profit of around Rs 0.8 billion. A discounted cash flow (DCF) valuation at a 10 per cent discount rate implied that the market was valuing the business at 2 per cent growth as compared to its track record of a 30 per cent past growth. It was a low-risk way to be exposed to high-quality cash-generating business with good growth prospects. The lubricant business had a promising future market strategy. It planned to:

1. make its products attractive to retailers and automobile mechanics;
2. add two or three automobile OEMs every year and to increase its presence in the business-to-business (B2B) segment;
3. introduce high value-added products to customers in the transportation and construction segments.

The demerger had a record date of June 2014. After the stipulated date, the shares of the GOCLCORP traded the ex-lubricant business. The GOCLCORP's other business was listed at a market capitalization of Rs 8 billion. I sold my GOCLCORP shares, as I had no interest in the businesses it owned. The lubricant business was listed in July 2014 as a separate entity at a market capitalization of around Rs 13 billion. The value unlocking was immediate. The two businesses separately were worth Rs 21 billion (8 and 13, respectively) vs Rs 10 billion as a combined entity. Thus, their market capitalization doubled through the spin-off process. However, coincidentally during this time, there was another major macro-trigger which supported the value unlocking—the May 2014 general election which resulted in the victory of the pro-reform Bharatiya Janata Party (BJP) government. Since then, the entire Indian market has been in a frenzy and has been rising as if uncoiling many years of burden.

CONCLUSION

No themes can be predetermined as sure shots. They are but a hunting ground where the landmines are fewer than usual.

Nonetheless, they are still there. A demerger theme is no exception. While it offers lucrative opportunities, it is not free of pitfalls. Mandhana Industries, Omkar Specialty Chemicals and Sintex Industries are poster boys of demerger themes that have gone wrong. Interestingly, these three companies have many similarities amongst themselves. The primary parent business is the commodity type, with a high debt and bad corporate governance. However, each of these parent companies owns relatively younger businesses which exhibit high growth, margins and RoE (based on pre-demerger financials) which it then decides to spin-off into a separate entity to be listed. Post the spin-off, most of the debt is retained by the parent company. The parent soon goes into a debt crisis. It is remarkable that the bankers gave the nod to demerge when the parent was saddled with debt. Surprisingly, in all the cases, the spun-off entity also showed weak revenue growth and net profit post the demerger—raising questions about the reliability of the pre-demerger financials. The whole episode resulted in the net shareholders' wealth destruction. This episode highlights the fact that weak corporate governance and a weak balance sheet does not create wealth, even if such businesses resort to demerger.

4

FROZEN FLAMINGO—SECTOR IN DISTRESS

Recession is opportunity in wolf's clothing.

—Robin Sharma, leadership expert

The Andes Mountain houses the largest colony of flamingos. At 40,000 feet above the ground, the temperature at night in the Andes falls low enough to freeze the alkaline lakes housing the flamingos. With frozen water around their legs, the flamingos' feet get trapped in the icy lakes. All they can do is patiently wait all night for the morning to come. Eventually, when the morning sun thins the ice the flamingos start to attempt to break free. It is still a struggle, but a few flamingos set themselves free and start to walk on the thin ice. Through the intermittent slipping and struggle, the flamingos resume their daily routine. Finally, when the ice melts away they press the reset button and start living again in the present—merrily feeding, dancing and mating, only to be trapped in the same icy lake again as night falls.[1]

Winters in the animal kingdom offer many such examples of temporary obstacles. Some animals migrate to warmer climates, and others burrow deep underground to hibernate until spring. Wood frogs of Alaska seek cover under leaves near the surface, where they go through multiple, consecutive freeze and thaw cycles over the course of the winter as the temperature outside varies considerably. During this period, the wood frogs stop breathing, and their hearts stop beating for weeks. In fact, the frogs' physical processes—from metabolic activity to waste production—grind to a near halt. Nevertheless, they resume normal, healthy living once winter passes by.[2]

To the unacquainted, frozen flamingos and frozen frogs are presumed dead. It is even easier for the frogs to be declared dead, as they are not even breathing! Similarly, coming back to the world of equities, we often come across sectors, which are going through their cyclical lows and it may appear that there is no recovery in sight. Investors shun such sectors. There is no light at the end of the tunnel. The sector only delivers bad news. The companies within the sector report losses and capacity utilization falls, as does the operating leverage. Perhaps some become bankrupt and debt restructuring rises. They are the equivalent of frozen flamingos or frogs that have stopped breathing. The companies that have become bankrupt mean less competition for the survivors. Those survivors emerge stronger and enjoy the rise in market share once the crisis is over and the cyclical upturn resumes. However, investors still shun it. Why? Before I answer that, let me discuss a few related incidents to better understand the underlying dynamics.

ART: PERCEPTION OR REALITY?

It was 7.51 on a Friday morning, rush hour, at the L'Enfant Plaza station; a violinist positioned himself against the wall, next to a trash basket. From a small case, he took out a violin. Placing the open case at his feet, he threw in some dollars and pocket change as seed money, positioned it to face the pedestrian traffic, and began to play. In the next forty-three minutes, he performed six classical pieces and 1,097 people passed by. Only seven people paused to take in the performance, at least for a minute. Twenty-seven people gave the violinist some money, most of them did so while on the run. By now, some of you must have recollected that this is the famous experiment that was conducted by *The Washington Post* back in 2007.[3] The violinist was Joshua Bell. It was art without a frame. He played one of the most intricate pieces ever written with his Stradivarius violin worth US$ 3.5 million. Two days before, a performance by Joshua Bell sold out at a theatre in Boston and the seats averaged US$ 100. *The Washington Post* was testing 'whether, in an incongruous context, ordinary people would recognize genius'. The conclusion was a resounding, 'No'.

Similarly, British graffiti artist Banksy, whose socially conscious works have attracted six figures at auctions, offered his signed spray paintings for US$ 60 a piece at a street-side stall outside Central Park, New York. The stall was stationed next to other art pedlars selling reprints. An anonymous elderly man staffed the stall. The deal of a lifetime lured just three buyers who bought eight paintings worth a quarter of a million for just US$ 420. As these were displayed on the street, the passers-by doubted their quality. They presumed it was one of the many amateurish paintings available in the vicinity.

These experiments have wider applications. It confirms that most people are perception-driven and tend to take things at face value. They regularly ignore relevant, fundamental facts to derive conclusions, and rather consider irrelevant and peripheral trivialities.

LOBSTER: MANURE OR DELICACY?

Now consider an even more interesting and real perception play that ran over centuries and involved millions of people. Picture a lobster served on the table. Imagine the restaurant in which it is served and the diner having it. What do you see—most likely, the swankiest restaurant in a posh locality? Is it being eaten by a formally dressed diner rather than someone who turned up casually. After all, the lobster is an exotic indulgence.

However, the lobster was not always a delicacy. In the seventeenth and eighteenth centuries, they were so abundant along the Massachusetts and New England shoreline that they would wash up on shore in drifts up to two-feet tall. People got so fed up with lobster meat, that they stopped eating it altogether. The lobster quickly earned a reputation for being a hollow bottom feeder, willing to put anything in its mouth. Its abundance made it the least desirable food—considered garbage, meat fit only for the indigent, indentured and incarcerated. John J. Rowan, in his book *The Emigrant and Sportsman in Canada: Some Experiences of An Old Country Settler* shed some light on how unworthy lobsters were during those times. He wrote, 'On still summer nights, lobster spearing parties are the fashion among Halifax people... On one occasion, I saw several acres of potato ground manured with them.' He added, 'Lobster shells about a house are looked upon as signs of poverty and degradation.' Perception rules. The meat quickly became synonymous with the lower classes of society and was mocked. The meat was so tainted that indentured servants in one Massachusetts town successfully sued their owners in order to limit the number of times the owners fed them with lobster meat. It was then limited to three times a week, at the most. Aaron Thomas's *History of Newfoundland* revealed that lobsters were a sort of universal feed for settlers' livestock, including fowl, cows, ducks, goats, geese, cats, horses, calves and pigs. Back then no one ever talked about its rich taste; its taste was eclipsed by the perception of lobsters as tainted, garbage meat.

Similarly, salmon was plentiful and cheap in England. Near the river, merchants fed their apprentices with it so frequently that they revolted and a law was passed limiting salmon lunches to two or three times a week.[4]

The lobster's tainted image changed gradually. The trigger was coal. Not in terms of a barbecue, but as the fuel that powered steam engines. By the late nineteenth century, enterprising railway companies rebranded lobsters as an exotic dish, and served them in dining cars on their trains. Also, from the 1870s onwards, the rise of seasonal tourism from New York and Washington to Boston saw lobsters becoming a sought-after item. Visitors, upon returning home from their vacations, would find themselves still craving Boston baked beans and boiled lobster. And they were willing to pay handsomely for it. External demand led to the popularization of canned lobster and eventually resulted in the development of the Maine fishing industry. On the supply side, overfishing started gradually reducing the supply, and the conservation laws of the 1940s further curtailed its supply and started to push the lobster prices up.

PRICE BEGETS VALUE

To return to our earlier question: Why do investors shun sectors that are in distress? Well, it is for the same reasons passers-by on a subway station ignored Joshua Bell, or the lobster was treated as garbage meat. There is a confluence of biases at play, which taints the perception of people. Let us look at each of them, one by one:

Social proof[5] bias made passers-by ignore Joshua Bell, as almost *everyone else was ignoring him*. People similarly adhered to social norms of staying away from the lobster. Investors stay away from distressed sectors as they are out of fashion and everyone abhors them. In other words, our perception affects our decisions.

Consistency and status quo[6] bias made passers-by ignore Joshua Bell as well. It is *consistent with their past action* of ignoring pianists in the subway. The same bias made the people of Maine treat the lobster as garbage meat for centuries. Moreover, the very same bias makes people ignore the distressed sector even when the sector starts to see green shoots.

Incentives[7] bias taught people to ignore subway pianists as paying any heed to them in the past would not have met their expectations. Similarly, the people of Maine were incentivized to shun the lobster or else put their own reputation at stake. Similarly, distress sectors are out of momentum and provide no incentives for the investors to buy them.

Mere association[8] bias is another factor the lobster was associated with garbage meat because it was given to servants and was used to feed animals; Joshua Bell was mistaken as an ordinary pianist as he was playing in a subway; and the distress sector with worsening financials seems a dead sector, with no hope of any return. Investors forget that it is a cycle and financials start to improve as the cycle turns.

Confirmation[9] bias made Maine people ignore the lobsters' sweet and briny taste as it disproved the status it held as garbage meat. Similarly, green shoots of a distressed sector are ignored as it disproves the initial hypothesis of the sector being dead.

To sum it up, these biases together make people ignore street musicians or distressed sectors. It was only the appreciation by railroad diners and travellers from other cities—external, unbiased influence—that gradually led to the change in biases towards lobsters.

Further, it becomes difficult to act rationally, as biases and the reality seem perfectly apt at that moment. For instance, the lobster's association with the lowly was justified by giving the lobster the reputation of a hollow bottom feeder, willing to put anything—no matter how barely edible—into its system. Today when the lobster has become expensive and is considered a delicacy, people only talk of its flavour and its exotic nature. Today, we hear everything that justifies the high price we pay for it. The same is true for sectors in distress. The grim and depressing sector news flow justifies investors avoiding them. Market prices are known to discount future events but, in the case of distressed sectors, market prices only reflect the current challenges. Thus, cyclical sectors tend to have cyclical share prices.

In essence, perception determines the price one pays. Joshua Bell and the lobster, were freely available and were therefore perceived to be worthless. A distressed sector is cheap, and its market price is mistaken for its value.

To overcome perception bias and see things the way they are, you have to start from scratch. It is necessary to look objectively at the data or the situation while ignoring the common perception and the current price. You must then collect enough evidence and try to connect the dots—only then can you conclude objectively and independently without any influence. The key is to start from scratch and to verify everything objectively while cutting through the noise.

CYCLICAL REAL ESTATE

Much like gold, the residential real estate in India is considered a store of value and has attracted smart, dumb, black and white money alike. Nonetheless, it has retained its cyclical characteristics, like anywhere else globally. Well, real estate is so popular for its cyclical characteristics that Jones Lang LaSalle (JLL, one of the top-notch property consulting companies) represents the state of the real estate market in various cities by plotting them on the circumference of a circle and popularized it as a property clock:

twelve o'clock represents the market peak, six o'clock the bottom. Each city strictly moves around the circle in a clockwise fashion and its position represents the condition of its real estate market.

Figure 4.1: Asia Pacific Office Property Clock (Q2 2019)

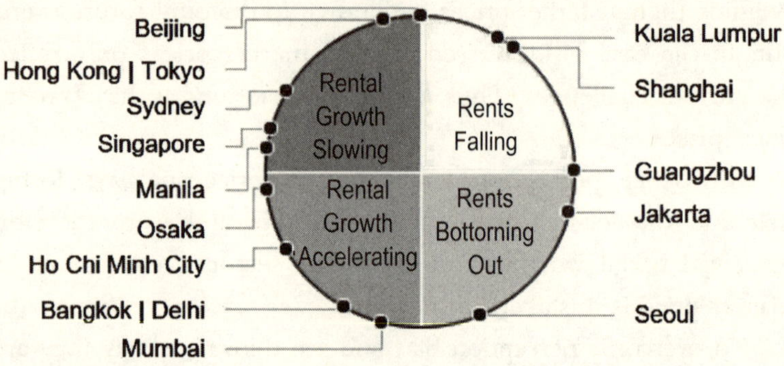

Quadrants of the clock:
- Top-left: Rental Growth Slowing
- Top-right: Rents Falling
- Bottom-left: Rental Growth Accelerating
- Bottom-right: Rents Bottoming Out

Cities (left side, top to bottom): Beijing; Hong Kong | Tokyo; Sydney; Singapore; Manila; Osaka; Ho Chi Minh City; Bangkok | Delhi; Mumbai

Cities (right side, top to bottom): Kuala Lumpur; Shanghai; Guangzhou; Jakarta; Seoul

Source: Jones Lang LaSalle (available at http://www.ap.jll.com/asia-pacific/en-gb/research/property-clock, accessed on 23 September 2019)

The key question is why is real estate cyclical? Well, for two reasons.

First, it takes a few years to build real estate. Most of the actual projects start only when higher demand outstrips supply and pushes prices higher. As no central authority controls the supply, it keeps on rising until prices start to fall and then the price itself acts as a natural supply breaker. However, by then enough committed projects have already begun and cannot be rolled back fast enough in response to the falling price. Moreover, projects that are off the ground would already have developer's equity committed to it (developer's equity thus becomes a sunk cost) and debt funding approved by the lenders. Thus, there is no incentive for the developer to roll back the project. This ensures the steady supply of unwelcomed projects, even when the prices continue to fall. Rising unwanted supply keeps pushing the prices lower for the next few years until rising population and subsequent demand clears the inventory. Andrew Lawrence, a property analyst at Dresdner Kleinwort Wasserstein in January, 1999, floated an innovative concept called the Skyscraper Index which showed that the world's tallest buildings have risen on the eve of economic downturns. Seeds for such ambitious projects are sown when the going is good and is expected to continue in the same manner in the distant future. These projects have a long gestation period. By the time the projects are actually delivered, the boom has already run its course and the economy is staring at a recession (to correct its past excesses).

A few notable examples of the tallest buildings in the world alongside the time they were built may help to illustrate the argument. The construction of the Chrysler building from 1928 to 1930 was the harbinger of the 1929 Great Depression; construction of the Petronas Towers from 1993 to 1996 and the Asian financial crisis in 1997; construction of the Burj Khalifa from 2004 to 2009 almost signalled 2009's great financial crisis. These are prime examples of how supply excesses get built during the easy-going days, giving cyclical characteristics to the sector.

Second, real estate is necessary as there is no substitute for land and housing. Therefore, when the sector is in shambles, we can be rest assured that it will bounce back as over time demand and supply rebalances. Only when the downturn becomes structural, real estate may not come back, as in the case of US shopping malls. The rise of Amazon (e-tailing) has sent many of the malls packing. US shopping malls lost their cyclical characteristics as the market structure has been altered by a technology-driven disruption in the retail sector. Residential real estate has yet to see a structural downturn in any country. It is strictly cyclical as the population keeps on rising and there is no substitute for land and housing. As demand gradually rises and outstrips excess supply. In a few decades, unless their immigration policies change, most developed and some emerging countries may see a fall in population which could bring on a structural decline for residential real estate in those countries.

Indian Real Estate: A Study

Since 2003, after almost a decade of sideways movement, residential real estate prices witnessed a stellar rise across Indian cities. The trend was supported by improving the global and local economies. Since 2005, regulation allowing foreign direct investment into the sector further supported the trend. But the 2008-09 global financial crisis quickly reversed this cycle, albeit, temporarily, as there remained a perennial deficit of housing units in India. Some estimates place the shortages at approximately 20 million plus units. The shortage is more than the population of most countries. Beginning in 2010, the rise of global liquidity and the improvement of India's economic condition started to revive residential real estate demand. Lower prices, post 2008-09 correction, increased affordability and attracted buyers in bulk. Prices and sales volume started to rise quickly and attracted developers with new launches, like bees to a honeypot. By 2011-12, rising speculation pushed prices high enough to hurt affordability—even in a country where buying a home has always been more of an emotional decision. Projects under construction rose, and sales started to slow down.

In 2013, the Indian economy started to slow down due to lack of reforms and private investments. Government actions remained inadequate. High oil prices raised India's current account deficit and weakened the currency. Consequently, imported inflation rose. The central bank raised interest rates to contain the inflation and that further affected housing demand—as housing loans became expensive. Nonetheless, despite a slowing economy, real estate prices broadly remained range-bound, with some downward trends.

From mid-2014 onwards, economic conditions have started to improve but the pile-up of unsold inventories has been large enough to keep the real estate sector struggling. Transaction volumes continued to fall. Unsold and underconstruction inventory rose across cities. Some cities fared better than others, but the downward trend was prevalent across the country. Slowing sales and downward drifting prices started hurting the developers' balance sheet. New project launches as well as progress on existing projects slowed down. Developers' revenue started to contract and profits shrunk. The only thing rising was debt and interest cost. Demonetization in end-2016 further delayed recovery. By 2019, small developers exited the sector and the real estate prices have stabilized. Demand for the affordable and low to medium-end properties have started to see improvements. But high-end properties continued to struggle. From 2013 to 2019, the Indian real estate sector has gone through a downturn and a stabilization phase. Real estate still is a classic example of a sector with pronounced cyclicality. Thus, post the stabilization phase, a cyclical upturn should return.

In the 2013-17 listed equity bull run, while most sectors were basking in the sunshine, most of the realty sector stocks remained the underdog. They were equivalent to frozen flamingos. Unlike the flamingos, the realty sector takes years to rebalance. Yes, such a long time can incite even a market-pro to throw in the towel.

MICROFINANCE INSTITUTIONS: RAPID GROWTH SOWS THE SEEDS OF A CRISIS

Microfinance institutions (MFI) in India started in 1974 with the establishment of Shri Mahila Sewa Sahakari Bank. The intent was to provide formal financing access to the rural unbanked population. It would then provide livelihood, promote entrepreneurship, eradicate poverty and raise financial inclusion. However, activity in this sector remained muted until the late 1990s. Until then, even though the interest rate in rural micro lending continued to be far higher than for large loans, the small size of lending made it inefficient for large banks to operate in such sparsely populated areas. Thus, most of the poor and rural population continued to rely on informal and unorganized moneylenders. Consequently, they were extorted like Antonio in Shakespeare's *Merchant of Venice*. Such financial exclusion has been debilitating for the poor.

Though financial inclusion has been progressing slowly in India, in 2001, 65 per cent of Indians were still unbanked. From 2001 to 2005, microfinance started to gain traction and saw its first phase of exponential growth. Annual growth in outreach reached up to 50 per cent[10] in 2004 and 2005 due to the low base effect. However, while the industry was advancing, it was also sowing the seeds of an upcoming crisis. The administrative capacity remained inadequate. Corporate governance and transparency were lacking, management information systems (MFIs) were poor. Amidst all this, loan books and clients grew rapidly, and MFIs attracted private capital which further accelerated the need for even faster growth to meet the return expectations of the new capital. Consequently, MFIs charged punitive and inflated interest rates and provided riskier loans. Different MFIs provided multiple credits to the same borrowers and finally resorted to coercive measures to recover their loans. This was most prevalent in the Krishna district of Andhra Pradesh in 2005. Local politicians raised voices against the MFIs and closed fifty-five branches operating in the region. Though the crisis was contained, the banks stopped lending to the MFIs for six months.

Equity investors injected liquidity into the cash-starved MFIs from mid-2006 onwards. The sector resumed growth as MFIs were the only channel of rural financial inclusion. Equity investment in the MFIs rose from US$ 6 million in the fiscal year 2006 to US$ 390 million in the fiscal year 2010.[11] Additionally, the government provided a priority sector tag to MFIs. This ensured that there would be no dearth of funds from banks to MFIs to meet their priority sector lending requirement. Growth was back. Between the years 2007 and 2009, MFI branches, field staff and the loan book more than doubled. The loan portfolio grew approximately twelve times during this time.[12]

But stellar growth is always followed by crisis. It occurred first in a few districts of Karnataka in 2009 and then spread across Andhra Pradesh in 2010 and 2011. It occurred due to similar reasons as was seen during the 2005 to 2006 crisis of the Krishna district in Andhra Pradesh, such as excessive risk-taking, multiple lending, coercive collection practices and high interest charges. Political intervention was again the trigger for the crisis. The Andhra Pradesh government without any warning issued the Microfinance Institutions Ordinance 2010 which raised administrative hurdles and placed stringent restrictions on the interest rate charged, and the collateral and method of loan recovery.[13] Consequently, MFI players' loan write-offs rose significantly and new loans disbursement came to a halt. MFIs en masse defaulted on bank loans.

Rural India cannot live without MFIs and financial inclusion must continue. To manage the situation, the Reserve Bank of India intervened and issued a detailed set of regulations to govern the operations of MFIs. New regulations were issued that capped multiple lending, interest rates, the leverage assumed by MFIs, loan per borrower, non-income generating loans, disbursements and recovery practices, among others. The priority sector lending status continued, and MFIs were to be regulated by credit information bureaus or self-regulatory organizations which were specially designed for such a purpose.

Have all these regulations made MFIs foolproof? No one can know with certainty but MFIs have resumed their growth. They grew roughly at a rate of 30 per cent CAGR (cumulative annual growth rate) between the fiscal years 2012 and 2016. Staffing in branches, equity investments into MFIs, clients and disbursements show similar growth statistics. Traditional markets have started to saturate and MFIs are venturing into unknown markets. MFIs have shifted their focus from the rural hinterland to urban pockets (> 2/3rd of lending). Non-bank funds, especially mutual funds now provide 40 per cent of funding to MFIs which have reduced reliance on traditional banks.[14] A few of them have converted into small banks (Bandhan, Ujjivan, Equitas, etc.) and Bharat Financial Inclusion merged with Indusland Bank. This reduced their vulnerability. But, other stand-alone MFIs remain vulnerable. Will there be another MFI crisis? Possibly. If it so happens, will the MFIs return to gain after a tough patch? For sure! MFIs are structurally very important for rural India, and they will come back to life, like the frozen flamingos.

CYCLES, CYCLES EVERYWHERE, LEAVING NO RETURN TO HOLD

Traditionally, commodities and real estate are both considered cyclical sectors. If you look deeper, the economy and stock markets would similarly be influenced by many cyclical factors. These factors make many sectors cyclical, although they make some sectors more cyclical than the others.

Table 4.1: Most of the Sectors are Cyclical

Cyclical Factors	Rationale	Sectors That Become Cyclical
GDP growth	Discretionary consumption and business capex (greed/fear driver) are cyclical	• Cement; capital goods; manufacturing; commercial vehicles; professional B2B services; logistics; • Luxury goods
Liquidity and sentiment	Cyclical GDP growth makes monetary policy and sentiments cyclical	• All sectors; • Financial services (stock broking, microfinance, NBFC); • Sectors dependent on frequent capital raising
Supply and demand mismatch makes pricing cyclical	Long gestation in bringing supply online	• Commodities and real estate • Commodity/oil as revenue or cost: airline, petrochemicals and plastics, rubber • Real estate aligned sectors: cement; building materials
Technology and patents	Technology innovation and obsolescence; patent expiry	• Technology, pharmaceuticals, biotechnology
Nature (weather)	Nature is unpredictable (intensity of rains and summer temperature; disease among animals)	• Agriculture commodity (including sugar, seeds, chemicals); agriculture machinery; rural-driven consumer businesses; horticulture; aquaculture • White goods (fridge; air conditioners; coolers)

Source: Author

Key takeaways from Table 4.1:

- Most stock prices are cyclical. Even if the earnings are defensive (that is utility or healthcare or consumer

staple businesses), the price to earnings ratio (P/E ratio) is cyclical as it is dependent on cyclical liquidity. Price (cyclical) = Earnings (defensive) * P/E (cyclical)
- Buy cyclical sectors under distress as they do come back to life. However, remember to sell when they get expensive as the winter night will return.
- The key exception is companies whose products have become obsolete. This phoenix may not necessarily rise from the ashes as it can be a structural issue.
- Businesses are cyclical, but the incompetent and unethical qualities of the management are mostly structural issues.

STOCK MARKET RETURNS REVERT TO MEAN

Figure 4.2 highlights the annual capital returns from the S&P 500 Index during 1928-2019. The returns are anything but linear. Cyclicality is the reality of stock markets. If you cannot beat cycles, join them. Acknowledge cyclicality and invest in the stock market accordingly.

Between 1970 and 2017, the S&P 500 Index has undergone eight corrections of 19 per cent or more from the all-time peak. The earliest was in 1970, and the latest was in 2008. Notably, two of the corrections were between 19 and 20 per cent, the correction of 1990 and 1998. Do note that equity markets technically enter a bear market when the broader index corrects by 20 per cent or more.

The index was trading close to its last twenty-year historical average P/E ratio during six of the past eight corrections. The remaining two times, during the dotcom bubble of 1998 and 2000, the index's valuation was extremely excessive (the index was

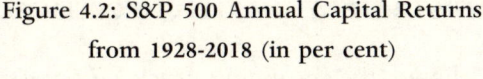

Figure 4.2: S&P 500 Annual Capital Returns from 1928-2018 (in per cent)

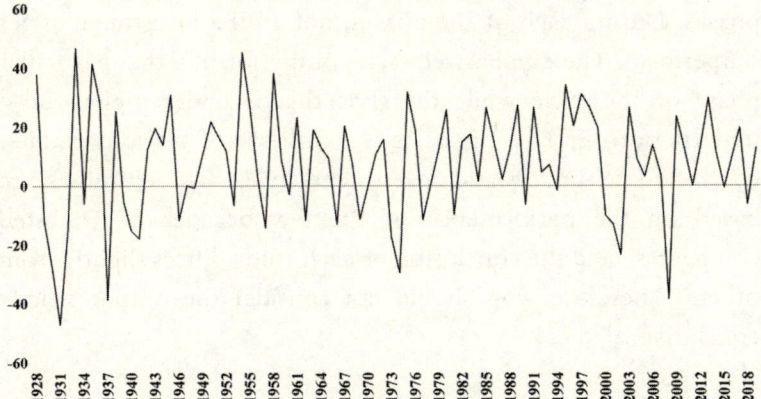

Source: Prepared from Capital IQ data (available at www.capitaliq.com, accessed on 22 July 2019)

trading 60 per cent higher than the historical average P/E ratio). In the six past instances when the market was not excessively valued, if an investor bought the index at 19 per cent correction and held on to it for ten years, the compounded annual total returns for the ten-year hold period would be a minimum of around 8 per cent and a maximum of about 19 per cent. In December 2018, the index was trading at its 20-year historical average and fell between 19 and 20 per cent. We will know by end-2028 how the index fared.

This trade set-up of buying S&P 500 index at 19 per cent correction and holding it for ten years, assuming the index is not trading significantly above its past twenty-year historical average P/E ratio, is one of the many ways to benefit from the stock market cyclicality.

INVESTMENT STRATEGY ADAPTED TO CYCLICAL REALITIES

Figure 4.3 shows the economic cycle progressing in four phases. During each of the phases, not all the investment styles outperform. The emphasized styles outperform in that particular phase of the cycle while the style that is underemphasized—underperforms. The figure is a synthesis of various studies conducted to understand investment styles. These studies are based on the performance of the few decades of US-listed companies', and the conclusion of each study differs slightly from others. Therefore, you should not consider the output strictly conclusive.

Figure 4.3: Preferred Investment Style

Early/Recovery	Mid-Expansion	Late-Expansion	Recession/Contraction
Value	Value	Value	Value
Momentum/Growth	**Momentum/Growth**	**Momentum/Growth**	Momentum/Growth
Quality	Quality	**Quality**	**Quality**
Small size	**Small size**	Small size	Small size
Low volatility/High yield	Low volatility/High yield	Low volatility/High yield	**Low volatility/High yield**

Source: Adapted from factorinvestor.com (available at https://www.factorinvestor.com/blog/2016/6/1/a-factor-investors-perspective-of-the-economic-cycle, accessed on 22 July 2019)

Nonetheless, a few observations can be made:

- No one particular style outperforms across all phases of the cycle.
- Quality outperforms in three of the four phases, and so quality stocks fit the 'buy and hold' investment philosophy.
- High dividend yielding stocks only outperform during the recession phase.

- Small cap stocks are the best bet post-recession but need to be exited before the start of the late-expansion phase so as to retain their outperformance.

To conclude, possible investment strategies based on investment styles are:

- Buy large capitalization quality companies and hold them for long-term periods.
- Buy small capitalization quality companies available at value prices at the start of recovery and sell them once economic expansion matures, that is, enters a late-cycle expansion.

5

DOLPHIN MUD-NET—BEFRIEND UNCERTAINTY

Volatility actually is the opposite of risk. It's an opportunity. But you need to think through and fight some basic human weaknesses.

—Jeffrey W. Ubben, co-founder, CEO and CIO, ValueAct Capital

Bottlenose dolphins of the shallow Crystal River and Florida Bay in Florida have devised a smart strategy to catch fish effortlessly. One of the dolphins beats its tail hard down the seabed in order to stir up the mud. While doing so, it swims circularly to create a ring of mushrooming mud, or a fishing net made of mud. The dolphin continues to swim inwards in a circular fashion to tighten the noose around the trapped fishes. As the mud-net begins to grow tighter and tighter, the agitated fishes only have one way out. They have to jump over the muddy net and into the air with the hope of landing back into the placid water out of the net. However, so much for their innocence, they fall straight into the gaping mouth of the many dolphins who have been lying in ambush outside of the net.[1] By this strategy, the dolphins successfully exploit the fishes' aversion to uncertainty, that is, mud-nets. Dolphins have brains as capable as those of humans. Consequently, many biologists speculate that they are as intelligent as humans. I bet that dolphins can outsmart most of us.

Humpback whales in southeastern Alaska have devised a bubble-net strategy which allows the harvesting of herring (a type of forage fish). Whales work in tandem and exhibit an extraordinary level of intelligence and cooperation, similar to the dolphins. The lead whale breaks from the group and dives down first. He is the bubble blower. It is his job to find a school of herring. The rest of the group follows. Once the leader has located a school of herring, he circularly swims beneath them and blows bubbles, encircling the group of herrings. A ring of bubbles, a bubble-net, starts to rise gradually towards the surface. Another whale sends a loud horrifying sound to prepare the whales. Panicked by the deafening sound and the blinding bubbles, the fishes do not cross this fizzing air bubble ring. Instead, they swim up to the surface and start jumping into the air while remaining trapped within the bubble-net. This creates a boiling effect on the surface. At this point, the whales swim into the bubble-net and reach the surface with their vast mouths open, scooping up their catch. Humpback whales in Alaska and Bryde's whales in the Gulf of Tosa, Japan, are the only two types of whales that feed on fish through this strategy.

Fishes tend to display a heightened vigilance in the face of uncertainty. They jump into the air to escape a perceived danger in the water. There is a similarity between the trapped fishes jumping over the mud-nets to the uprooted insects discussed in Chapter 3. Here, mud-nets are the trigger. However, the critical difference between the two strategies is that while faced with the mud-net, fishes have a choice—whether or not to jump. Dolphins don't force them to jump—they simply create a situation that prompts the fishes to jump directly into their gaping mouths. In this sense, the fishes are duped. However, in the case of insects, the choice is just not there. They are beaten by a dominant force and are forced to move. They cannot stay still. What this means is that the trigger as described in Chapter 3 is a more predictable and bankable strategy in yielding food.

Unfortunately, humans too make hasty decisions much like fishes in order to avoid uncertainty. Studies have shown that humans choose to receive an electric shock in the present moment than assume that they could be subjected to one later.[2] In addition, these studies have shown that the participants exhibited greater activation in their nervous systems, while they were waiting for an unpredictable shock than when receiving one. Greater activation in their nervous systems increased their systolic and diastolic blood pressure, reflecting heightened vigilance and physical discomfort. Thus, many a time we conduct irrational acts to reduce an uncertainty, thereby reducing the physical pain we may experience during an uncertain time.

To understand the implication of 'uncertainty aversion tendency' on financial decisions, Benedetto De Martino of the California Institute of Technology in 2006 ran a study with twenty university students. Each was given US$ 50[3] and made to play two games.

For Game A, they were asked to choose between the following two options:

1. keep US$ 30, or
2. gamble with a 50/50 chance of losing the whole money.

What would you have done? Of the participants, 43 per cent decided to gamble.

For Game B, the participants were again asked to choose between two options:

1. lose US$ 20, or
2. gamble with a 50/50 chance of keeping the whole money.

HOW WOULD YOU HAVE RESPONDED?

To avoid losing the entire amount, the number of participants who decided to gamble rose to 61 per cent (the difference between the participants' probability to gamble in the two games is statistically significant). In Game A, a majority of the subjects were risk-averse in front of a sure US$ 30. While, in Game B, the majority became risk-seekers and preferred to gamble to avoid losing US$ 20—highlighting the loss aversion mindset. Most of the participants did not realize that in both games, not choosing to gamble would mean walking home with US$ 30.

The following section highlights the creative exploitation of this loss aversion tendency when uncertainty is involved in financial decisions. We do not have to go to a con artist show to observe how people stuck with loss aversion tendency part with their money. This exploitation is regularly evident in the capital market.

TIGHTENING MUD-NETS IN CAPITAL MARKETS

In capital markets globally, investors exhibit a loss aversion mindset to the market's uncertainty, that is, a mud-net. Various macroeconomic and company-specific forces (dolphins in this case) create these mud-nets. Normally, the frontal lobe of the human brain is responsible for reasoning and decision-making. But, when we are up against unexpected and unfamiliar risks, the amygdala hijacks our frontal lobe and takes over the decision-making functions. The amygdala is an almond-shaped set of neurons located a few inches from each ear. It provides us with our most primitive instincts: fear, hunger and arousal. It has served our forest-dwelling ancestors well by initiating flight or fight response when faced against a predator or while in search of food or shelter.

During uncertain times, the amygdala activates first and then decides on the flight or fight situation, that is whether to jump (sell) or to not jump (hold) the mud-net. Most of the time, the amygdala directs the investor to sell in the falling market to avoid the pain of losing money. Assuming that the investment's fundamentals remain intact, some investors do manage to think from their frontal lobe and hold on to their investments. But the decision to hold may not be absolute. As more investors throw in the towel, the persistent selling pressure further pushes down the price. Tightening mud-nets further incites even more investors to exit the company. At this stage, investors begin to doubt their understanding of the company and its fundamentals. Irrelevant, bearish views take precedence. Such a tendency is especially true in the public markets due to diffused and/or low ownership. Diffused ownership results in infrequent management–shareholder communication, thereby resulting in the investors assuming an unclear and mostly negative picture of the business. Share prices are assumed to reflect the health of the company and falling share prices give way for negative news to gain prominence. Consequently, many long-term investors also bail out. During such periods, the price is determined by irrationality and fear. This vicious cycle of falling prices and investors' selling continue until the stock finds its bottom. Falling prices form a base when the stock has fallen significantly compared, thereby attracting buyers. By that time, the security is mostly held by investors who are either numb to losses or truly believe in the fundamentals of the stock. In the first case, the investors have muted their amygdala, and in the latter case, they are thinking through their frontal lobe.

To examine the role of the amygdala when faced with monetary losses, Benedetto De Martino conducted a series of experimental tasks on two individuals with focal bilateral amygdala lesions. He asked the participants to play a variety of games with possible gains and losses. He concluded, 'Although both participants retained a normal ability to respond to changes in the gambles' expected value and risk, they showed a dramatic reduction in loss aversion compared to matched controls. The findings suggest that the amygdala plays a significant role in generating loss aversion.'[3]

Scientists have conducted experiments on rats to study anxiety. Rats have a lot to be anxious about with ample predators and minimal defence. They inserted thin wires into rats' brains to remove their amygdalas. Removal of the amygdalas took away their memory of fear, including that of cats!

Thus, we can conclude that damage to the amygdala, which governs the emotions, makes people behave more rationally, while making decisions. Their choices stop taking emotional processes into account. The obvious question to ask is how to switch off the amygdala while faced with an uncertain financial situation or monetary losses. Fortunately, we do not have to pierce our amygdala with wires to tame it.

TOLERATING MUD-NETS: TAMING THE AMYGDALA

I tackle uncertain situations by finding solace in the Bhagavad Gita's fundamental teaching, 'Karmanye Vadhikaraste Ma Phaleshu Kada Chana'. It simply means, 'to do one's job without worrying about the outcome'. The Gita preaches the benefits of being calm under both pleasure and pain. Consequently, I focus on picking fundamentally sound stocks after extensive in-depth research. Once

I have invested, I practise patience. Irrespective of your religious orientation, practising detachment from the results and staying dispassionate can help anyone stay calm and tame the amygdala when surrounded by uncertainty. In fact, even trying to detach yourself will yield significant benefits. To quote Ajay Piramal of Piramal Enterprises, 'My greatest learning from the Bhagavad Gita is that if you are dispassionate, you will win.'[4]

Ask yourself, would any of this matter in 1,000 years? Even Buddha has said that everything is temporary. So why fret? Ironically, this relinquishment helps me stay more in control. Yes, complete detachment is quite challenging. But it is worth the attempt. Ray Dalio, the founder of a renowned investment firm, Bridgewater Associates, meditates twice daily. He said in an interview to the CNBC, 'Transcendental Meditation has probably been the single most important reason for whatever success I've had', and added, 'It helps slow things down so that I can act calmly, even in the face of chaos, just like a ninja in a street fight.'[5]

Another way to manage uncertainty is to imagine the worst-case scenario. Therefore, when the worst does materialize—it becomes a lot more bearable and does not come as a shock. In the documentary, *Becoming Warren Buffett,* Buffett shows Berkshire Hathaway offices and explains the decor. Buffet says, 'Originally, when I moved in 1962, you can see this (pointing to a few paintings), I went down to the South Omaha Library, and I think for a dollar I got seven copies of old, *New York Times* from big times like the Panic of 1907,' he said. 'This one, 1929, obviously,' he said, pointing to a paper on the wall that marked the beginning of the Great Depression. 'But I wanted to put on the walls days of extreme panic in Wall Street, just as a reminder that anything can happen in this world,' Buffett adds, 'I mean, it's instructive art, you can call it.' These pieces of art acknowledge market risks, provide courage to face them and remind him that bad days do pass and better ones do follow. Even stoic philosophers from Greece advocated premeditation as a strategy to reduce reactionary tendencies and to soften the blow of unwanted situations. Essentially, this acknowledgment and pre-planning lowers the shock when risks materialize. Thereby, it avoids irrational decisions driven by the amygdala.

CAUTIOUSLY EXPLOITING MUD-NETS: ONE MAN'S TRASH IS ANOTHER MAN'S GOLD

In the capital markets, you regularly have to face mud-nets. It becomes your job to decipher them. If you are in the net, then you have to decide if it is time to fold your cards or merely stay put or buy more. A thumb rule here is to check if the fundamentals of the company remain intact. If they are, then you need to hold on to it, or possibly, even buy more and wait for the mud-nets to dissipate—which they eventually will.

Conversely, and fortunately, if you are out of the net then the question is whether you should exploit the situation by jumping into the net by buying the shares of the company. If yes, then at what price? First, you have to determine if fundamentally the company is attractive. The challenge is that during uncertain times, the fundamentals themselves become questionable and bearish views start to float around. During such times, I repeatedly look for companies that have an 'easy to quantify' safety net. The safety net becomes vital during such times, as it will provide a backstop to the worst-case valuation and market price—ensuring that you do not catch a falling knife. This leaves significant room for upside when sanity arrives and market conditions improve.

Multiple factors provide this safety net to a company's valuations. They are:

1. Free net cash or fixed income-generating asset
2. Management quality
3. Business quality

Figure 5.1: The Three Safety Net Factors Represented as a Venn Diagram

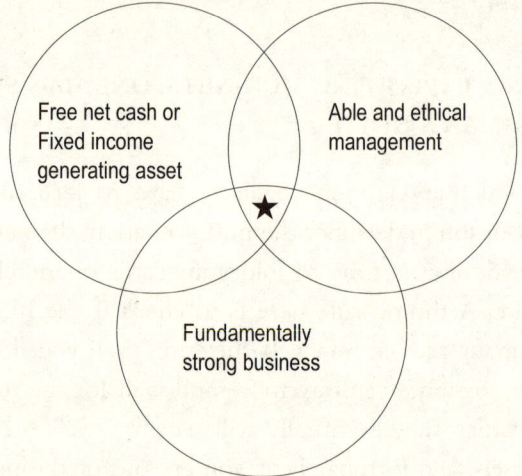

Note: The star indicates the sweet spot, i.e., one should find companies which have all the three components as shown in the three circles.

Source: Author

Of these three, the first is most tangible and least debatable. An ideal combination would be to have a company with this tangible safety net as well as a fundamentally strong business—both run by an able and ethical management. Indian markets have often presented fundamentally strong business run by able and ethical management, sitting on free net cash that is worth more than the market capitalization of the company (effectively turning the enterprise value, that is, the sum of market capitalization and total debt minus cash in the company of the company negative). There was a plethora of companies in 2009 trading at negative enterprise value. Notable recent examples are Force Motors (2012) and Piramal Enterprises (2011/2012) among others.

Interestingly, sometimes the market also provides a combination of two businesses within the same company—a fixed income-generating asset and a fundamentally strong business with a significant upside. Both are run by the same able and ethical management, and are available below the value of the fixed income-generating asset. It therefore provides the other fundamentally strong business and able management free to the shareholders. This theme is one of my favourites as it can be most rewarding with a minimum downside. Moreover, the presence of a fixed income-generating business is preferred over cash, as cash can be spent away unproductively. Following are a few examples to understand how I have tried to put all this into practice.

TECHNO ELECTRIC AND ENGINEERING COMPANY LIMITED (TECHNOE)

Between 2011 and 2013, India's investment cycle collapsed like a flan in a cupboard. Quarterly net fixed investments[6] fell to Rs 784 billion as compared to an average of Rs 4,850 billion per quarter during 2007-09. Structural issues and policy logjams in heavy industries led to the investment slowdown. At a global level, during mid-2013, the US Federal Reserve's Taper Tantrum (the attempt to buy fewer bonds from the markets, thereby raising US interest rates) strengthened the US dollar. A strong US dollar and the high oil prices weakened Indian rupees and raised domestic inflation. The RBI tried to control inflation by raising interest rates. This ended in hurting private consumption and capital expenditure. Capacity utilization fell across capital goods industries. Uncertainty around the outcome of the impending general election of 2014 further subdued the sentiment.

For a stock picker, the mud-nets created by various dolphins were too thick to escape. The mud-nets were caused by the US's Taper Tantrum and domestically, by weakening currency, rising inflation, rising interest rates, slowing demand, falling capacity utilization, slowing investments, order books and the impending general election. Nevertheless, such times produce some of the most exciting opportunities. I was frantically looking for mud-nets that I could see through that the markets could not. Primarily, I was looking for companies whose stock prices were beaten down to the point that there were no or limited further downside, but a massive upside whenever these mud-nets would have dissipated.

It was during this time when I bumped into TECHNOE. In September 2013, TECHNOE was available at a market capitalization of around Rs 4.7 billion. Founded in 1963, it provides end-to-end solutions for the construction of power plants. It has been involved in the commissioning of over 50 per cent of India's thermal power-generation capacity and in setting up a significant portion of the National Grid. Well, its laurels end here. In 2013, its order book fell to 1.7 times sales or almost one-third lower than its 2010 order book. The order book determines the future revenue visibility. Thus, the market seemed to have rightfully punished the stock.

Its infrastructure division was solid with a robust execution capability, track record and customer relationship. However, during bearish times, the price fall may continue, as the timing of cyclical recovery is uncertain. Fortunately, TECHNOE also had a 207 MW windmill division that had a twenty-year power sale agreement with Tamil Nadu's state electricity company.

Table 5.1: TECHNOE's Financials

Fiscal Year 2013 (Rs Billion)	Combined	Infrastructure	Windmill
Market capitalization	4.7	–	–
Net debt	6.7	–	–
Enterprise value	11.4 (4.7 + 6.7)	–	–
Revenue	6.8	4.9	1.9
Net profit	1.2	0.4	0.8
Fair market value of equity (after deducting net debt)	12.2 (8.5 + 10.4 – 6.7)	8.5 (10x of last 4 yr avg. PBIT)	10.4 (Replacement value)

Source: Techno Electric and Engineering Company Ltd Annual Reports 2013 (available at http://www.techno.co.in/AnnualReport.aspx?Name=Techno, accessed on 22 July 2019)

As shown in Table 5.1, TECHNOE then was trading at a market capitalization of Rs 4.7 billion and the combined enterprise value of the firm was Rs 11.4 billion. In contrast, the replacement cost of building the 207 MW windmill itself was worth Rs 10.4 billion (Rs 50 million/MW). Thus, the well-run infrastructure division with three decades of a steady track record and good customer relationship was almost available for free. As shown in Table 5.1, the conservative fair market value of equity was at least Rs 12.2 billion or roughly 2.6 times upside to the then market capitalization.

In 2013, Indian economy was close to its cyclical lows. There was a high chance of the pro-reform Modi government coming to power. This would kick-start capital expenditure in the power sector. Moreover, TECHNOE is one of the better players with a strong track record and clean corporate governance. It is known for its control on overhead costs, bidding discipline and efficient working capital management.

Let us pause here. If you had encountered the above situation—what would you have done? Every investor who knew of TECHNOE then encountered this question: Would you have gone ahead and bought this company in your portfolio? If yes, please pick one from the reasons below that would have convinced you to swing your bat:

1. cheap valuations and expected cyclical recovery;
2. strong infrastructure division available for free, providing an upside when the cycle turns;
3. stable windmill-operating business providing downside protection;
4. twin businesses: one providing a significant upside for free with the other protecting the downside.

All these are valid reasons to buy the shares of the company. Nevertheless, there were many companies in the similar space, available very cheaply and who would benefit from an expected cyclical recovery. The principal reason to purchase this stock amidst gloom was the twin businesses that TECHNOE provided. The renewable operating business with a twenty-year power sale agreement in place was protecting the downside, while the infrastructure division, available free, could be worth multiple times the then market capitalization of TECHNOE.

Fortunately, I did not have to wait long. In May 2014, the incumbent Congress party lost the election, and the pro-reform BJP government won. Market and economic sentiments improved consequently. TECHNOE's order book jumped to Rs 26 billion by March 2016 (versus Rs 8.5 billion in September 2013). The revenues, profit and cash yield from the infrastructure division staged a sharp comeback. The fiscal year 2016 net profit from the infrastructure division rose to Rs 1.2 billion compared to the average net profit from 2010 to 2013 of Rs 0.7 billion. Market capitalization in April

2017 rose to approximately Rs 46 billion (Rs 4.7 billion in September 2013, a ten times rise during this period). By early 2017, it became fairly valued and since the risk reward was not attractive any more, I exited the stock. To conclude, the micro and macro mud-nets of 2013 were nothing but perceived risks, and they presented a rewarding opportunity for those who patiently considered the facts. I could tame my amygdala-driven, fear and built my convictions to buy the stock.

PTL ENTERPRISES (PTL)

In the middle of 2013, I found another company called PTL Enterprises (PTL) while randomly reading various annual reports. The various macroeconomic mud-nets, which we saw in TECHNO's case, also made PTL attractive. PTL had two divisions. One division had a bond like revenues and cash flows and provided a critical safety net. The other division was the future growth engine of the company which was available for free.

PTL is an associate company of Apollo Tyres Ltd and is run by Onkar Singh Kanwal, chairman and MD of Apollo Tyres. Kanwal has helped Apollo Tyres grow from a small, single plant unit into a large global corporation with revenues of Rs 172 billion plus. Rarely does one get capable management running a small capitalization company like PTL. PTL had two different businesses: a tyre manufacturing facility located in Kerala, leased to Apollo Tyres Ltd.(tyre business); a healthcare facility delivered via Artemis Health Institute, Gurgaon.

I was attracted to PTL's tyre business, which had an annual contractual lease revenue of Rs 400 million from Apollo Tyres and Rs 367 million of operating profit before tax. The lease started in March 2006 and had a contractual maturity in March 2022.

Table 5.2: PTL's Financials

Fiscal Year 2013 (Rs Billion)	Combined	Tyre Business	Healthcare Business
Market capitalization	1.2	–	–
Net debt	1.7	–	–
Enterprise value	2.9 (1.2 + 1.7)	–	–
Revenue	2.6	0.4	2.2
PBIT	0.52	0.37	0.15
Fair market value of equity (after deducting net debt)	1.9 (2.1 + 1.5 − 1.7)	2.1 (10% discounting of PBIT till lease maturity, 2022)	1.5 (10 times of PBIT implying no growth and 10% discount rate)

Source: PTL Enterprises Limited Annual Report 2013 (available at https://www.bseindia.com/stock-share-price/financials/annualreports/509220/, accessed on 22 July 2019)

I conservatively attributed the value of the lease to be Rs 2.1 billion while ignoring the terminal value of the leased space after maturity. To estimate the upside, assuming that the lease is extended to infinity at Rs 400 million per year, its discounted value would rise to Rs 3.7 billion. The tyre business was valued at between Rs 2.1 and 3.7 billion. Against this, the company had an enterprise value at Rs 2.9 billion.

The PTL's healthcare business then was almost available for free. It was like a lottery ticket, one with a substantial probability of hitting the jackpot. Its healthcare business consisted of the 300-bed Artemis Hospital in Gurgaon. By March 2013, it was approximately 50 per cent utilized and its revenue was growing at a CAGR of 19 per cent for the last three years. As shown in Table 5.2, 'Healthcare' and the 'Tyre Business' together resulted in a conservative equity value of Rs 1.9 billion against a market capitalization of Rs 1.2 billion—

implying an 1.6 times upside. Moreover, based on the private equity hospital deals at around Rs 20 million/bed, the healthcare business alone could be valued at Rs 6 billion.

Therefore, to me, it was a no-brainer prompting me to jump into the mud-net no matter how murky the market appeared to be. Post-September 2013, PTL's 'Tyre Business' remained steady. Healthcare business's revenue and profitability more than doubled by 2016. In February 2016, PTL announced plans to demerge its healthcare business into a separate entity called Artemis Global Life Sciences. By May 2019, the combined market capitalization rose to roughly Rs 6.3 billion, approximately a five times jump in five years.

THE OTHERS

Force Motors (FORCEMOT.BO) is a forerunner of the large commercial vehicle industry in India. It is well known for its brands. Its market capitalization in 2012-13 was below its free cash in the books. Then, even after significant research, I could not understand what it would do with its cash. By May 2019, the stock rose five times. The rising demand for luxury cars in India turned the tide for Force Motors. Since 1997, it had produced engines for Mercedes cars made in India. It built its future on the back of this business. In 2015, Force Motors set up a new facility to build engines for BMW cars produced in India. In 2016, it inaugurated a new plant to increase the production capacity of its Mercedes engines. Consequently, net profit rose more than ten times between 2013 and 2019. Force Motors is a classic example of buying a quality business with a minimum downside despite limited clarity on its future direction, and patiently wait for it to show its mojo.

In 2013, Smartlink Holdings Limited (SMARTLINK), a no-debt company, was available at a market capitalization, which was 50 per cent of the net cash in the books. But the challenge was that its

IT network product business was struggling to cope with cheaper Chinese products. It did not have any plan to use the idle cash. But the cash was real, the management was ethical and would often reward minority shareholders with buybacks and dividends. It almost doubled in the next five years, and the management is yet to find good use of its cash.

QIHOO 360 TECHNOLOGY CO. LTD

Listed in the US in 2011, Qihoo is one of the largest Chinese antivirus software companies. By 2015, its founder CEO Zhou Hongyi wanted to privatize and relist the firm back in China to extract better pricing as the US equity markets were underpricing the Chinese companies.[7] The company's strategic importance to China also called for domestic listing. However, events leading to the privatization faced a thick mud-net. It was the largest Chinese company proposed to be privatized at a valuation of US$ 9.3 billion.[8] Large size became a hurdle as billions of US dollars had to be moved offshore from China, where Qihoo's money was, to complete the transaction. This became a challenge as China, in mid-2015, upped restriction on offshore transfers. Adding to the uncertainty was the news that Chinese regulator signalled it would slow or even halt the use of a backdoor listing path that many companies are using to relist back home—post privatization in the US. This obstacle was rumoured to prompt CEO Zhou to promise assured returns to his investors backing the privatization if Qihoo was not relisted within a certain period. I am sure, you are already feeling quite dizzy. Yes, the mud-net was thick enough to see through.

The plot thickened further. In mid-2015, the CEO did not give forward guidance in the quarterly conference call as he said that he was working towards privatizing the company. To me it was a very strong sign of privatization materializing. However, the street took this gesture very negatively, and by September 2015 pushed the market capitalization of the company down to around US$ 5.5 billion. The P/E ratio of the company was lowered to around twenty times. For the company, which has doubled its revenue every year in the past, it was cheap. In 2015, its revenue was expected to grow by around 30-40 per cent. And its net profit margin was expected to continue to expand. So the fundamentals were strong and valuation was compelling. Privatization at US$ 9.3 billion, if successful, would return around 70 per cent. The likelihood was high as the CEO, along with its investors, were already controlling 61 per cent of the market capitalization. Therefore, the funds needed to privatize were not excessive. Alternatively, the market was giving the opportunity to buy at a cheap price, shares of a fast-growing company with a leadership position in the cyber security sector that has a strong macro tailwind.

Finally, in December 2015, the CEO gave a firm offer to buy the company at US$ 9.3 billion. The company was taken private in July 2016. Between December 2015 and March 2019, the company's net profit rose almost 80 per cent. It was relisted in China in February 2018 and in May 2019 had a market capitalization of approximately US$ 20 billion. In hindsight, privatization was probably not the best outcome for the Qihoo US shareholders.

TAKEAWAYS

To conclude, during uncertain times such stocks with downside protection should provide enough confidence for investors to buy in large quantities. During bearish and uncertain times, investors are more concerned about how low prices can drop and therefore, stocks with downside protection are a more comfortable buy. Moreover, in such times, the market tends to not price in the growth prospects, and so, often the future growth comes free. Lastly, if we were to draw parallels, the examples of TECHNOE,

PTL and Qihoo are in spirit, similar to Warren Buffett's deal to buy US$ 5 billion of preferred stock of Goldman Sachs in late 2008, providing 10 per cent dividends. For this deal, Buffett received downside protection, that is preferred dividends and the principal was placed superior to ordinary equity shareholders in the capital structure. In addition, he received warrants worth US$ 5 billion with a five-year exercise period at a strike price of US$ 115/share—serving a sweet and significant upside.

6

CITY MONKEYS—FINDING MANNA IN A NEW TERRITORY

In general, great companies prefer to grow 'organically', as Wall Street likes to say. That is, from the inside out, by finding new markets or by taking market share from their competitors.

—Alex Berenson, former *New York Times* reporter

For most animals, venturing into the city comes with its own hostilities. Nevertheless, to the bold, it ushers in surprising opportunities. Mandore Garden of Jodhpur, India, which houses Hindu temples and ancient monuments, reveals the surprising relation between humans and Hanuman langurs—monkeys named after the Hindu god, Hanuman. Langurs are revered here, and this guarantees a constant source of food for them. A high-energy diet has led to baby boomers, with the female langurs reproducing twice as fast as their nearby forest counterparts. Twins are common here, but a rarity in the wild. Because of the less time spent looking for food and the absence of predators, langurs drop their guard and spend most of the time playing. The rewards of living in the city can be huge. The challenge is to find your niche.

In the quest to experience the many benefits of nature, we often overlook what is available in our cities. Just as the human population has adapted to city life over the centuries so have many species of wildlife. In fact, cities may become hotbeds for studying animal evolution in the future—perhaps an urban Galapagos is in the making.

New York City's Staten Island has been visited by a new species of bird called the osprey—also called the sea hawk or river hawk or and fish hawk. In fact, more ospreys are nesting in North America than ever before. Ospreys have forsaken trees in favour of building their nests on power poles, cell phone towers, channel markers and other man-made structures. Ospreys have learned to tolerate people, and are even raising their young next to busy highways or marinas. Crows too have been using US cities to their advantage. They are known for dropping bones and nuts from great heights to crack the tough, outer shells to extract the food inside. The black-crowned night heron, an endangered bird, has its biggest colony in the heart of Chicago. The bird is adapting to urban spaces, and proving that cities can be a conservation ground.

Not only birds, but animals are also benefitting from the life of a city. Coyotes (a species related to the dog and wolf) are now common in Chicago. They are very resilient and adaptable. For example, they have so acclimatized to the city that they understand traffic flows while crossing the street and easily find places to use as dens, unnoticed even in the busiest areas. According to Ohio State University professor Stan Gehrt, a coyote living in Chicago has a 60 per cent chance of surviving another year, while a rural coyote has only a 30 per cent chance.

Cities provide a steady temperature, abundance of food sources, limited competition and few predators. Thus, urbanization, even though it has been forced, has been proven to be a movement towards greener pastures for some animal species who can find their niche in the city. Well, good for them but are we benefiting from their presence? The answer depends on social and cultural connect. In the Ethiopian city of Harar, the hyenas that hang around the streets in the night perform 'ecosystem services' by munching street rubbish, as do the vultures that fly over Indian cities. Similarly, pavement ants, insects and spiders consume a big portion of the junk food tossed on the ground in New York City. Whereas in Rome, wild boars are seen as a nuisance, as a motorbike rider died after hitting one.

Well, city dwelling is not for all species. Only 8 per cent of native birds and 25 per cent of native plant species are present in urban areas. Moving to greener pastures is challenging. Most simply cannot survive or have never dared to venture out.[1]

IT IS ALL ABOUT FOREX

Moving to greener pastures for manna continues to transform the lives of individuals, companies and countries in aggregate. China since 1991 has found its manna in export-led growth strategy and has become the 'factory of the world'. China's exports by value have risen to match up to that of Japan and Germany. The export binge has consistently boosted trade surpluses, forex reserves and the currency value. Strong external finances have created room for easy monetary policies to fund domestic infrastructure and the boom of heavy industries. Their bulging economic muscles have significantly elevated the country's stature in global geopolitics, and the International Monetary Fund (IMF) has designated its currency to a reserve status—same as the dollar, pound, euro and yen. Yes, the tag 'Made in China' comes with a reputation of its own but it works for China. McDonald's works too, even as it serves junk food to its customers—serving the masses is the trick.

Similar to China, but on a smaller scale, other European and Asian countries have built their economies around exports of goods and services to counter their reliance on oil imports. Prominent ones are Singapore, South Korea, Taiwan, Ireland, the Netherlands and Switzerland. Well, India is not far behind. 'Make in India' is a step to further this trend. However, will we succeed? Only time will tell, but it will be a very slow and uphill task. Please note that I am not including commodity-exporting countries. Yes, their manna comes from other countries' pies, but their efforts are comparatively simpler—they happen to have the mineral resources and have just had to export it at prevailing prices.

Trade is a modern way to eat into our neighbour's pie. Well, it is better than the Mughal invasion of India or Europeans stealing land from Native Americans (American Indians), or even European and British colonialism—history is generously sprayed with barbaric attempts to grab the other neighbours' share. Historically, revolt has been the reply to invasion and colonialism. Today, tariffs are the reply to international trade, especially to protect the domestic industry. Drawing a parallel with the langurs in India, city authorities who have received enough complaints from the residents sent specialized men to trap nuisance-creating city monkeys and take them back to the jungle, some 150 kms from the city of Jodhpur.

Other impressive forms of tapping into a neighbours' pie are inbound tourism ventures and citizen migrating abroad and sending remittances back home. In the last decade, Dubai and Thailand have done a wonderful job of attracting a non-stop tourist flow from India. Similarly, most of the island countries in the Indian Ocean and the Caribbean rely heavily on revenue from tourism. Coming to migration, globally, twenty-five countries receive at least 10 per cent of their GDP as remittance from their citizens working abroad.[2] In fact, closer home, remittances from citizens working abroad form 30 per cent of real GDP for Nepal, and roughly 6 per cent for Bangladesh. Mexico has almost 12 per cent of its native-born population living overseas, mostly in the US. Rising emigration from the Middle East and Africa into Europe is an uncoordinated and en masse search for greener pastures.

PARADIGM SHIFT—THE NEXT BIG THING

In the last two decades, Indian pharmaceuticals and technology sectors benefitted from rising generic drug export and technology offshoring trends! While animals and individuals have to physically migrate to a new territory to find manna, corporates often come out with innovative strategies beyond simple exports, to tap into the neighbour's pie to find manna. It broadly involves one of the following strategic steps:

- Enhancing revenue: through exports or by adding new revenue streams.
- Expanding margins: moving up the value chain such as a B2B company moving into business-to-consumer (B2C) space.
- Changing the management set-up: better management that can bring about new strategic direction and transformation.

Such moves promise a bounty. Can you guess what is common among Apple, Amazon, Netflix, TCS and WIPRO? Yes, they all are technology companies and are successful. But more importantly, they all have diversified on their way to the top. Apple started with personal computers in the mid-1970s. When it could not compete with Intel and Microsoft it diversified into newer products with iPhone being the latest. Amazon started as an online book retailer and netflix as a rental video website. The Tata Group's first company was Indian Hotels Company (1902); their most valued TCS came much later in 1968. WIPRO started as Western India Vegetable Products Limited selling vegetable oils.

But diversification comes with risks that are associated with unknown territories. The risk can be contained by allocating a small portion of the capital to the new business; injecting incremental capital as things start to work out. Some of the best examples of Indian companies under this theme are below:

Domestic demand play: Founded in 1984 as a branded watch retailer, Titan Company diversified its revenue stream into branded jewellery (Tanishq) in 1994 to counter a rising, stiff competition in its watch retailing space. Tanishq has remained the leader in its category since then. By 2002, jewellery sales have exceeded that of watches and have become the core business of the company. Between 2002 and 2019, Titan's total revenue increased roughly twenty-nine times, net profit rose approximately 107 times and share price rose almost 300 times.[3] Titan enhanced its revenue, expanded its margin and became a true compounder for its shareholders.

Price differential driven exports play: The automobile sector has had its share of companies that have ventured out to find manna and have gotten plenty of it. Founded in 1975, by the early 2000s Motherson Sumi Systems Ltd (MOTHERSUMI) was a No. Two supplier (only after Bharat Forge) of auto ancillary products and services to automobile companies. Known for its quality products, some 18 per cent of its revenues came from exports. In 2002, it found its 'aha moment' when it opened its UAE operations in Sharjah to cater to the global markets. Since 2002, its exports have grown consistently and have clocked almost 50 per cent CAGR and by the fiscal year 2019, exports have been almost 85 per cent of its total revenue. During these seventeen years, net profit grew ninety-five times (to Rs 16 billion) and share prices grew 220 times[4] (to Rs 360 billion). Through this time, MOTHERSUMI leveraged the cost differential of producing the auto ancillary in India vs the US (10-20 per cent cheaper) and Europe (50 per cent cheaper).

Classic brand play: Founded in 1948, Eicher Motors Ltd (EICHERMOT), in a joint venture with Volvo, has been manufacturing commercial trucks and buses. It owns the Royal Enfield motorcycle business. First built in 1901, the Royal Enfield Bullet is the longest-lived motorcycle design in history. In 2000, it was making a loss and EICHERMOT decided to revive it, give it one final chance after multiple such chances had failed. It took many years to fix the technical issues. In 2008, Royal Enfield launched its newly designed 500cc Classic model in Germany—inspired by its J2, a 1950 model Bullet. It was a success, admired for its performance and fuel economy. In 2009, it launched a 350cc bike, priced at Rs 1.20 lakh. This proved to be a hit too. By 2010-11, the tide had turned, and all minor issues were resolved. Sales rose, and capacity utilization hit 100 per cent (from 33 per cent in 2000). Order backlog piled in so much that customers had to wait for six months to receive their orders. Gradually, it ramped up its capacity utilization and with it rose its share prices—jumped almost twenty-five times[5] between 2010 and 2019. This period coincided with the rising GDP growth in India and rising consumer aspirations and it made room for indulging in classic luxury at twice or thrice the price of regular motorbikes. EICHERMOT's manna came from its brand's legacy which was till then lying dormant in its backyard.

Each of the above three companies from the very beginning have been leaders in their space. These leaders were best suited to capitalize on the trend. However, their market capitalization remained modest as the market could not see its growth far into the long run due to their strategic change in direction. The market ignored the size of the new opportunity, which was much larger compared to the existing company itself. The new opportunity would have raised the possibility of significant value creation, if the company delivered. From the investors' perspective, the market offered a good risk-reward scenario. A decade-long growth opportunity was available with little to lose if the new manna-producing businesses did not ultimately materialize, as the investors were barely paying for it. Titan's manna came from the rising domestic demand for branded jewellery; MOTHERSUMI's from rising exports of auto ancillary products; EICHERMOT's from a rising demand of domestic luxury, legacy bikes. It is crucial to note that an investor does not have to be an early entrant into such businesses. Taking stock after the businesses have proved their worth can also be significantly rewarding. In all the above cases, it is only after the business is proven with limited uncertainty, that the significant rerating took place.

More recently, Reliance Industries, the refinery and petrochemical giant, foray into retail and digital space is one of the most grandiose pursuits of manna in the new territory.

Below, let's look at a few live examples of companies which are moving to greener pastures in search of manna.

BALAJI TELEFILMS—AN INDIAN NETFLIX IN THE MAKING?

Balaji Telefilms (BALAJITELE) is known for popularizing the family soap opera culture in India since the late 1990s. BALAJITELE produces almost 1300-1400 hours of TV show content every year.

In 2017, the company started making web-series (also known as Over The Top, OTT) and distributing them to viewers through its app called Alt Balaji (Alt). OTT has already proven itself to be a successful model in the West, with key players such as Netflix, HBO, Hulu, Disney and Amazon. Alt, if executed well, could change the structure of BALAJITELE from a B2B player to a B2C player, selling content directly to the consumers.

The market for OTT is huge. India has more than 150 million households with a TV connection. Of these, 114 million households have a cable/satellite connection and 37 million households have Direct-To-Home (DTH)[6] TV connection—all these households are already paying monthly for home entertainment and are thus potential customers of OTT. Well, the OTT market size is bigger, especially as OTT is enjoyed individually (and not as a household).

BALAJITELE's management quality, its focus on OTT and its deep understanding of Indian media provides hope that its OTT business can become as successful as its TV show business. Yes, the competition is rising and that is the key risk. However, providers with good content quality should prevail. The only way to approach such opportunities is to buy at a price where the downside becomes very limited, while the upside remains huge.

In mid-2019, it was trading at around Rs 50 per share or at a market capitalization of Rs 5.3 billion with net cash and short-term investments in the books at about Rs 3.2 billion. Therefore, the enterprise value was only Rs 2.1 billion.[7] Against this, the company is a contender to grab decent market share in the sunrise OTT industry of India, and has a TV business as a cash cow, throwing around Rs 0.2-0.3 billion net profit annually. Therefore, the downside looks limited.

Wockhardt Ltd (WOCKPHARMA), after years of selling generic drugs, is now close to having its own branded formulations. It has been working on them since the mid-1990s, and has spent Rs 30 billion[8] plus over the years on new drug discovery, R&D, which it has conservatively charged against its profit and loss account. Currently, it has five of its New Chemical Entity drugs in advanced trial phases. The molecules are expected to cure serious, hospital-acquired infections. Possibly, as early as 2021, the company may start selling its first drug. Like BALAJITELE, WOCKPHARMA is also changing its structure and looks set to have a brighter future, as compared to its troublesome last decade. Additionally, like BALAJITELE, the WOCKPHARMA share price by mid-2019 does not even properly value the generic business, let alone the upside from the new drug discovery, which could be significant.

Founded in 1994, Rossell India (ROSSELLIND) is a tea plantation company. In 2010, the limited prospects of the tea business prompted Rishab Gupta, the third-generation scion, to seek manna outside the core tea business. That gave birth to a new business line of supplying components and parts to aerospace and defence companies. The company's willingness and attitude to learn earned ROSSELLIND Boeing's 'Supplier of the Year' award in 2015—only after two years of supply engagement. Now it is targeting new customers and is working on diversifying away from the wiring business and exploring opportunities in the defence maintenance, repair and operations (MRO) space.

Its aerospace and defence revenue base is small at about Rs 1.1 billion[9] for the fiscal year 2019, and the management has an order book of Rs 2.8 billion; it has ambitious plans for the future. With a sector tailwind, the cost advantage of manufacturing in India, Rishab's passion for aviation and the company's overall ambitious management plans, the future may be very different for ROSSELLIND. Importantly, the downside seems limited with market capitalization at almost 0.6 times of total consolidated sales.

In the US, the largest discount brokers—Schwab, Fidelity, TD Ameritrade, and Pershing—already control almost 62 per cent of the broking market. In India, however, discount broking is a new phenomenon. Multiple articles are written on how discount share broker, Zerodha, has been disrupting the stockbroking industry.

Zerodha started its discount sharebroking business in 2010, and charged a very low fixed commission on share trading while keeping their services to a bare minimum without any advisory and other ancillary services. In March 2019, Zerodha with an active client base at 0.9 million topped all the brokers in India. ICICI Securities has been pushed to the No. 2 position with 0.83 million active clients. The industry not only offers growth but also robust profits. Discount brokers' net margin can be as high as 35 per cent to 45 per cent once players attain full scale and start benefiting from the operating leverage that kicks in.

Although a late entrant, 5 Paisa Capital's (5PAISA) progress goes unnoticed. 5PAISA, a demerged company of the diversified, financial services company, IIFL Holdings, started discount broking in 2016. By March 2019, it became the No.2 player among discount brokers with an active client base at 0.1 million and a broking volume market share of 1.3 per cent[10] (Zerodha is at 15 per cent). Its revenue is growing very fast and in the fiscal year 2020 it can cross Rs 1 billion. The key risk is competition not only from Zerodha, but also from new entrant Paytm.

CHANGE IN OWNERSHIP

A lot of research has been dedicated to understanding the impact of a change in the company's management and its stock returns. There is no consistency, and the result depends on various factors such as geography, company size, industry, hold period, underlying stock market condition among others. Even if there were a clear correlation, it would be meaningless for individual, stock picking purposes—beyond providing illusory comfort.

The most bankable theme in the Indian markets since the 1990s is betting against government-managed companies. The two ways to play this theme are by buying:

- *A private company that has government company as its key competitor*: Government-owned HMT watches was the leader in watches until the 1980s. In 1984, the Tata Group-owned Titan Company ventured into watchmaking and steadily took the market share away from HMT. Similarly, in 1993/1994, a handful of private banks were set up, and since then public sector banks (PSBs) have been consistently ceding their market share to private counterparts. Between 2000 and 2019, share prices of these private sector banks have increased between 50 and 300 times versus twelve times increase in the share price of the largest public sector bank, State Banks of India. In 2019, the PSBs market share was roughly 70 per cent which only indicates that private banks will continue to grow and grab the market share away from PSBs.
- *Government companies that are getting privatized*: Privatization is positive for the minority shareholders as private management is expected to improve value creation. Prominent examples are three large companies that were privatized in India in the early 2000s: Videsh Sanchar Nigam Ltd (VSNL); Hindustan Zinc; Maruti Udyog. By 2019, Maruti Suzuki's name changed, and the share price rose almost forty times; Hindustan Zinc's share price rose more than hundred times; VSNL (name changed to Tata Communications) had limited value creation due to sector challenges. In comparison, during the same time, the BSE Sensex Index rose almost twelve times.

SAFARI INDUSTRIES (SAFARIND.BO)

In 2011, the headlines, 'Former VIP Industries MD Sudhir Jatia buying 56.55 per cent in Safari Inds', caught my attention. I sprang into action as it was clear that I had spotted what was possibly very interesting news. Safari Industry (SAFARIND.BO) then was a micro-cap loss-making company. However, its Safari brand was the third largest brand in a luggage industry, which was an oligopoly. The company had many loss-making stock keeping units (SKUs), product variety was restricted and consequently its revenue at Rs 0.7 billion was too small for the third largest player. In comparison, VIP Industries, the largest player, clocked Rs 7.5 billion in revenue that year. The second largest player, Samsonite, had revenues close to that of VIP. Regarding enterprise value, while VIP Industries was trading at Rs 27.5 billion (almost four times to sales), SAFARIND.BO was then available at one time sales. There was a lot of room for improvement in SAFARIND.BO's revenue, profits and valuations. Rarely do we find a micro-cap stock available with a known brand, which further has industry-leading management running it. Sudhir Jatia took a few positive steps. He discontinued loss-making SKUs, introduced products in the Indian army's canteen stores department and started e-commerce sales. He launched polycarbonate luggage and introduced new products such as laptop bags, school bags and backpacks. Consequently by 2019, sales increased by eight times[11] and share prices rose by almost twenty times.

UNIPLY INDUSTRIES (UNIPLY)

In 2015, something similar happened. I came across a discussion on stock in June 2015. This time it was Keshav Kantamneni. In Q2 2015, he bought around 36 per cent stake in Uniply Industries

Ltd. (UNIPLY). Keshav is a graduate of the Kellogg School of Management and comes from a business family. Through his family, he has held business interests in wood logging in Africa and ply doors trading. He also runs an investment banking firm Globality Partners. The UNIPLY promoter (a company's founder is commonly addressed as a promoter in India) approached Globality to sell their stake, and Keshav found this as a good opportunity to scoop the promoter stake of an established plywood brand and become a manufacturer himself.

In 2015, the total plywood market in India was roughly Rs 60 billion. GreenPly had 25 per cent market share, Century Plyboards at approximately 17 per cent, which left UNIPLY at No.3 with only about 2 per cent. The other players were very small. Keshav, in an interview mentioned that UNIPLY deserved a gain in market share, as the current share did not justify its third position. He further wanted to increase capacity utilization (40 per cent then), better source raw materials from Africa, expand the dealer network, build a brand and acquire a plant in north India to reduce transportation costs and retire high-cost debt.

In August 2015, renowned investors R.K. Damani, Ramesh Damani, Enam Investment Services and Sara Vallabh Bhanshali participated in a fresh equity capital raise. By 2019, Keshav had carried out most of his plans and the revenue almost rose $4.7x^{12}$ while the share price rose almost fifteen times since the new management took over.

Quoting Seth Klarman from his book *Margin of Safety*, 'Even if the present could somehow be perfectly understood, most investments are dependent on outcomes that cannot be accurately foreseen.' To the contrary, all the above situations entailed a change in management or the existing management entering into a new business line. This even makes the present tricky, let alone trying to predict the future. Detail forecasting and analysis are fruitless in such cases. The prevailing uncertainty would mean that most investors would be left sucking their thumbs (in UNIPLY that is what I did, and then I entered almost after the price doubled! Still, better late than sorry). Such a situation calls for an art of investing in its true sense, which comes only with experience. Nevertheless, following are the essential ingredients that may build confidence in investors for them to pull the trigger when they encounter such inherently, unpredictable situations:

- existing foundation to build the future on
  - a strong brand (Tata; Suzuki; Royal Enfield; Safari; Uniply),
  - low-cost but good-quality products (Motherson Sumi; Wockhardt's new drug discovery programme; Rossell India);
- large addressable market in value terms;
- 'execution' or management strength to see things through in the new environment; and
- limited downside.

Success for such companies is a matter of probability. Nothing is certain, as these companies are walking down uncharted territory. The management themselves are unsure of the future, but they still put their best foot forward. However, some of them have potential to surprise the investors in a couple of years. Therefore, the safest approach is to buy a handful of such manna-seeking companies, restricting allocation in the range of 3-5 per cent per idea. Continue to monitor the progress for say, two to three years and exit the ones that are not able to deliver while retaining and even buying more of the promising ones.

7

STARLING MURMURATIONS—CLONE A WEB OF INVESTORS

There is no harm being a copycat. If someone else is doing a great job, copy. It's free.

—Uday Kotak, CEO, Kotak Mahindra Bank

It is not only an abundance of food that attracts wild animals to cities. Cities are usually several degrees warmer than their neighbouring countryside. In Rome, in December, one species of animal takes full advantage of the city's extra heat. After feeding in the neighbouring countryside, starlings in the evening come to the city to roost overnight in their nesting trees.

Once they have arrived in the city—they must descend to the nesting trees, but the first ones to do so are at the highest risk of being caught by the predators (a first mover disadvantage is common in the animal kingdom). Therefore, they wait in the sky for the others to arrive. There is safety in numbers. As daylight fades, a staggering one million starlings fill the sky. They flock together and stay in sync performing spectacular aerobatics in the sky for some time. They continuously form dynamic and mesmerizing movements in various shades of grey over a sunset. To the imaginative mind, the constantly changing shapes may resemble anything: a country's map, a giant bird, a head-down image of a man, a swan, a foetus. Eventually, en masse they brave the descent, and fill the branches of their favourite trees. The next morning, they leave their mark while checking out, heading back to the countryside. During a single winter morning, ten tonnes of their droppings rain down on the city. They spare no one, from automobiles to garbage cans to roads and houses. On these cold winter nights, the city's extra warmth can be the difference between life and death.

The online journal, *Open Science*, simulated a computer programme to understand why starlings flock together.[1] The experiment simulated a three-dimensional flock of starlings with humans as predator hawks tasked to attempt to pick out one of the birds. The task became exceptionally challenging. Known as the confusion effect, the model starlings appeared to be safer from predation in bigger and denser flocks. Other benefits of the large flock are that more birds can be on the lookout for predators at any point in time. As news of a predator seeps through the group, it leads to the flock taking evasive action—visually appearing as a murmuration. For similar reasons, fishes swim together (called a schooling).

How do starlings flock together? Do they have a leader? In 2010, Andrea Cavagna and his team at the National Council of Research and the University of Rome used advanced computational modelling to conclude that starlings flock collectively without a leader. When any one starling changes direction or speed, the seven nearest neighbours coordinate the movement accurately (as per George Young at Princeton).[2] Every starling in the pack responds consistently and instantaneously to the neighbour's change in movement, resulting in zero error during the transmission—a significant advantage for a starling trying to dodge a falcon.

ETHNICIST

As birds flock together and fishes swim in schools, humans similarly form ethnic conclaves. Indians, living abroad, have formed groups in Jackson Heights in Queens (New York City), Edison in New Jersey, Mahatma Gandhi District in Houston, Wembley and Southall in London, Little India in Singapore, Brickfields in Kuala Lumpur, Deira/Karama/Bur Dubai in Dubai, Indian Quarter in Durban and in many more places. These are melting pots of Indian restaurants, shops and cultures, but are garnished with the influence of the global city in which they are located.

The Punjabi Indians dominate Southall in west London. So much so that the train station there is named in the Punjabi language. A few restaurants there even accept Indian rupees. Moving to east London, Brick Lane is a fascinating example of ethnic herding behaviour in sync with economic realities. It was a haven for immigrants moving to London to escape persecution abroad or seek the good life. The French settled there in the 17th century, then the Irish in the 19th century and the Jewish in the early 20th century. The Jews remained there until the mid-20th century. Subsequently, Jewish prosperity rose, and they started to move out, making way for Bangladeshis to settle in. This transition continued for a few decades and eventually today, everything there has been built and populated by the Bangladeshis—making it famous for its curry houses and nightclubs. Which ethnic group will replace Bangladeshis in a few decades? Time will tell.

Ethnic herding is not limited to South Asians. There are thirty-six Chinatowns globally, Binondo in Manila is possibly the oldest (established in 1594), and Manhattan Chinatown in New York City is the largest. There are multiple Koreatowns, Little Italy, Dutch villages and other ethnic conclaves sprinkled across the world—proving our collective behaviour.

Ancient Greeks call this tendency to associate and bond with similar others as the Homophily principle. Similarity breeds connection, builds strength and protects. This Homophily principle is prevalent in personal and commercial relationships and network ties of every type, including friendship, marriage, etc. Ethnic Homophily (Chinatowns or Southall) creates the strongest divide among individuals and is further centred on age, religion, education, occupation and gender—roughly in that order. Geographic proximity, families, organizations and social/psychological similarities (intelligence, attitudes and aspirations) all create contexts within which such homophilous relations form.

A homophily tendency conveys our likes and dislikes and defines us. It allows us to reflect upon our socio-cultural demographics, and our behavioural and intrapersonal characteristics. It also consequently, stereotypes us. The Diversity Visa issued by the US, and the Ivy League US business schools preferring candidates with diverse backgrounds for admission are ways to control the homophily tendency.

To the contrary, ties between non-similar individuals also dissolve at a higher rate, facilitating the formation of niches (localized positions). Brick Lane is a prime example as some 30-60 years ago the Jewish community gradually moved out as Bangladeshis prominence rose—progressively replacing the Jewish bagel and coffee shops with curry houses.

MAGNETIC CONVERGENCE

Ever wondered what is common between Silicon Valley, the banking centres in New York, London and Hollywood? Yes, wealth, but at a deeper level, it is an example of industrial flocking. Well, these are the crème de la crème examples of clustering. Other than them, globally, there are innumerable clusters—mostly small. In India, there are some 6,400 industrial, handloom and handicraft clusters. Industrial flocking is as old as industrialization itself. For example in the year 1350, the handloom cluster of Chanderi was established in Madhya Pradesh, and it is old enough to be mentioned in the Mahabharata. Similarly, the handicraft cluster of Moradabad bloomed in the 19th century, and the British took the art to international markets.[3] Alfred Marshall in 1890 highlighted the importance of industrial agglomeration. Then in 1990, Michael Porter in his book *The Competitive Advantage of Nations*, introduced and popularized the term 'industrial clustering'. In 1991, Paul Krugman also highlighted the importance of geographical economics.

Enough ink has been spilled in highlighting the reasons for industrial clustering, as well as detailing the performance advantages that clusters enjoy as compared to their stand-alone cousins. Some of the clusters happen as a result of historical accidents. But for most, they provide competitive advantages either by lowering the production cost (availability of cheap labour, or conducive natural resources, or proximity to clients or shared resources) or by providing access to technical know-how (technology firms). In the age of technology, a location should no longer be a source of competitive advantage. Ironically, the champions of technology themselves are clustered around Silicon Valley, as most of their important information comes not electronically, but through face-to-face meetings. Look around yourself—perhaps, there are some industrial clusters in the vicinity.

However, not all industries benefit from clustering. The ones that benefit are industries serving businesses such as mining, financial, information, communication, technology and professional services. Customer-facing businesses such as retail, healthcare, real estate, education and social work operate best when sprinkled everywhere.

Herding behaviour is also pervasive in geopolitics, power struggles and ideologies: World War II, the Cold War, Western countries extending sanctions against Iran or Russia, the Middle East tensions such as Qatar vs Gulf Cooperation Council (GCC) or Iran and allies vs Saudi Arabia and allies. They all are a clash of ideologies, which brings like-minded countries together and places them against other countries with an opposing mindset.

The crucial difference between the flocking of birds and humans is that the former lacks leadership while the latter often has one.

If a stock exhibits specific association then the homophily principle helps to decipher the stock's characteristics and attractiveness. Yes, I am hinting towards coat-tailing or cloning—as popularized by famous value investor, Mohnish Pabrai, but this is not a naïve coat-tailing, and there is lot more thought that goes into it.

CONNECT THE DOTS TO SEW A WEB OF INTERESTING LEADS

Companies regularly flock with the like-minded. Rarely will you see competent and ethical management in business dealings with a company that has an incompetent or unethical management. Thus, when a company with an excellent management enters into a strategic tie-up with another company, this other company immediately passes the quality management test and is worth analysing further. Conglomerates with recurrent inorganic and strategic tie-ups across various sectors provide excellent clues for a shrewd stock picker.

There are many renowned conglomerates with an ethical and able management, but I found Piramal Enterprises (PEL) quite interesting. Thanks to Sanjay Bakshi, whose musings on his blog brought PEL to my notice in 2012. Founder-Chairman Ajay Piramal is a sharp and well-regarded businessperson who has built enormous wealth for his shareholders through a series of smart acquisitions and monetization. In 2010, the company sold part of its healthcare business to Abbott Labs of the US for US$ 3.8 billion. The question to ask then was what Piramal would do with the cash. Therefore, I started tracking PEL. As it was free of legacy issues it would be deploying cash in attractive sectors and companies. The answer came quickly. In 2013 and 2014, PEL invested in Shriram Group's financial services business. In 2014, they entered into a joint venture with Navin Fluorine (NAVINFLUOR) to manufacture fluorochemicals (specialty chemicals) for its critical care business. In 2015, PEL started real estate financing in a big way. Further, Piramal and family's private company bought a stake in Sunteck Realty (SUNTECK).

These dealings drew my attention to financial services, specialty chemicals and the real estate sector. Specifically, NAVINFLUOR and SUNTECK were companies worth digging into. Piramal's commercial interest in these companies ensured that ethical and able management would run them (the homophily principle). This piece of information itself is quite useful, especially in the real estate sector where clean management can command a premium in an otherwise murky sector and transactions.

Moreover, the coat-tailing does not end here. Well, we have to sew the whole web. NAVINFLUOR's shareholding showed that Rahul Sarogi of Atyant Capital allocated a good chunk of his fund to NAVINFLUOR, since the third quarter of 2011. Further analysing Sarogi's portfolio highlighted his orientation towards ethical and competent management, long-term buying and holding strategy, few and concentrated bets aligned to long-term trends or an expected cyclical sector upturn.

To continue to sew the thread, we have to rope in Mohnish Pabrai, a renowned US-based fund manager, with concentrated investment bets in India. In November 2014, he bought GIC Housing Finance (GICHSGFIN), a few months after PEL acquired a 20 per cent stake in Shriram Capital. In June 2016, Pabrai invested in a specialty chemical company called Oriental Carbon and Chemicals (OCCL). The company manufactures and markets insoluble sulphur, sulphuric acid and oleum—for the tyre and rubber industry. The only other listed company manufacturing similar products is the National Organic Chemical Industries Ltd (NOCIL). Coincidentally, NOCIL's and NAVINFLUOR's chairperson are close relatives. Further, in early 2017, Pabrai bought a stake in two real estate companies: Kolte-Patil Developers (KOLTEPATIL) and SUNTECK. To recollect, Piramal's private company has invested in SUNTECK since 2015. Lastly, in May 2017, Pabrai publicly recommended PEL Enterprises as the 'Next Berkshire Hathaway Stock' to Warren Buffett.

The above web proves that like-minded people often also feed off each other (equivalent of the murmuration of starlings).

NAVIN FLUORINE (NAVINFLUOR)

In 2002, due to debt restructuring, Mafatlal Industries Limited (MAFATLAIND) carved out and listed NAVINFLUOR separately. NAVINFLUOR is one of the top three Indian players in fluorochemicals with over forty-five years of experience and forty plus commercial products. Fluorochemicals is a niche and specialized chemistry with very few players globally. Four of ten discoveries made in the pharmaceutical sector involve fluorochemicals. Approximately 20 per cent of all drugs in the market contain at least one fluorine substituent. Over the years, the company has gradually moved up the value chain by developing high-margin niche products, with a tight control on cost. It has expanded its offerings from the refrigerant to specialty fluorochemicals, to Contract Research and Manufacturing (CRAM), for third parties. From a technology and products vendor, it was gradually becoming a specialized research and services partner. NAVINFLUOR's CRAM business was enabling it to make a play on the outsourcing of drug discoveries by large pharmaceutical companies.

NAVINFLUOR's sharp focus on fluorination chemistry and strong customer relationships allows it to have joint ventures and tie-ups with best in class partners. Coming to the joint venture with PEL, NAVINFLUOR is supplying specialty fluorochemicals to the joint venture that will manufacture products with specific applications in the healthcare industry. Additionally, NAVINFLUOR has entered into supply and technology licences agreement with Honeywell International (HON), to produce next generation automobile refrigerants. These strategic moves are enabling it to move up the value chain and raise its profit margins.[4]

Back in mid-2016, it was available at a market capitalization of Rs 2.2 billion at a 25 P/E ratio. However, I estimated the fair value to be anything between Rs 3.2 and 5.0 billion, hinging primarily on the expansion of the EBITDA margin and growth of the CRAM business. The market capitalization in mid-2019 rose to Rs 3.5 billion with a P/E ratio of twenty-three.

SUNTECK REALTY (SUNTECK)

I have always admired Sunteck Realty (SUNTECK) for its marquee Bandra Kurla Complex (BKC) projects. It is a quality Mumbai developer with a strong balance sheet, and better management than many other companies in the sector. I started looking at SUNTECK in 2015, shortly after PEL bought a stake in it.

Founded by Kamal Khetan, a first generation entrepreneur, the company is backed not only by Piramal (4.6%) but also by the Kotak Group (6.5%)—two of the better names in the Indian corporate world. SUNTECK also has a 50:50 joint venture with the Piramal Group to develop projects in the BKC. In 2015, SUNTECK won awards from the Asia Pacific Real Estate Association for 1. best practices; 2. best property development organization; 3. best market disclosures and 4. best property valuation.

The BKC is the new central business district of Mumbai. It houses the headquarters of large corporations, financial institutions and investment funds. Office and residential property prices there have risen to match the growing fame of the location. SUNTECK is the only developer in the BKC. Since 2009, it launched 220 units spread across three high-end projects (Signature Island, Signia Isles and Signia Pearl) totalling 1.5 million square feet. By 2015, more than 60 per cent of the projects were pre-sold. Pricing was between Rs 40,000-55,000 per square feet. Exclusivity meets monopoly pricing. Financiers and industrialists who bought an apartment in one of SUNTECK's three projects were Uday Kotak, Gautam Adani, Vikram Pandit, Gunit Chadha, Nimesh Kampani, Harsh Mariwala, Jalal Dani, Kishore Lulla and Ashok Wadhwa.

SUNTECK's balance sheet stands out among its peers. In 2015, its net debt at Rs 7.9 billion was only 0.4x its net worth (0.7x for peers). Furthermore, its land bank was fully paid for. Around 75 per cent of the land bank is located in the BKC or Goregaon—within Mumbai city limits. The low cost of land has resulted in high margins, which are sustainable especially because the BKC's residential prices were expected to rise on strong demand. In the fiscal year 2015, its revenue was only Rs 3 billion and net profit was Rs 0.7 billion. Nevertheless, this should rise substantially in the next two to three years as Rs 14 billion revenues from pre-sales in the three BKC projects are recognized as the BKC projects get completed. Lastly, SUNTECK was expected to launch eight projects worth Rs 89 billion—most of them would be in Goregaon.[5] Therefore, the pre-sales are likely to continue to remain strong in the coming years as well.

On valuations, by the end of 2015, it was trading at a market capitalization of Rs 16 billion. I calculated the value of its BKC and other ongoing projects at around Rs 21 billion and its pipeline project at Rs 14 billion—a total of Rs 35 billion. Thus, SUNTECK then was available at almost a 55 per cent discount. This was a large cushion which would have tempted any investor to plunge in, no matter how bleak the sector outlook appeared to be. Further, I assumed that there would be no rise in residential prices in the next five years, which was conservative. I also ignored the land bank which had no monetization plan in the next three years. By 2019, its market capitalization rose to Rs 62 billion. I realized that human beings tend to be super-conservative in bearish times, especially when the margin of safety is exceptionally large.

THE CLONER: SALMAN KHAN

The continued success of Salman Khan, one of the most renowed, Indian actors of all times, has its foundation in cloning. He entered the film industry in 1988 and acted in a few superhits until 1999. However, the 2000s were a rough patch in his career. The turning point came in 2009 with the movie, *Wanted*, which was an official remake of the south Indian film, *Pokiri*. Since then he has been in a superhit movie almost every year, and most of them have been remakes of south Indian films. He has been in twelve superhit movies from 2009 to 2018—the most any actor has been in during this time. Most of those twelve hits were copies of south Indian movies. As it famously goes, 'Imitation is the sincerest form of flattery'. According to the Forbes 2015 list of World's Highest-Paid

Superstars, Salman was ranked seventy-first, the highest ranked Indian, with earnings of US$ 33.5 million. Salman had found a successful formula in cloning and now sticks to it, something many corporates could learn from.

TRENDSPOTTING

Most of the private equity players are growth investors. It would be rare to find value investors in the private equity field. Value investing only works in the public equity markets where inefficiency results in temporarily mouth-watering value prepositions. To the contrary, well-negotiated private equity transactions result in no party leaving obvious value on the table. Efficiency prevails. Additionally, private equity players have to raise money every few years, so they have to promise as well as deliver high returns. A brutal combination of the need for high returns in an efficient setting means private equity players have to frequent sectors and companies promising high growth. Well, it means a strong signalling effect for us. Sectors that start attracting a flock of private equity investors indicate their promising future growth prospects.

A few companies that were listed between 2015 and 2019 have been consistently experiencing very high growth. They are Quess Corp, Dixon Technologies, TeamLease Services, Dr Lal Pathlabs and Eris Lifescience. Private equity players backed all of them before they were listed. It must be kept in mind that private equity players have invested in duds as well. Nonetheless, in general, they have been quite right in spotting high growth sectors and companies. A remarkable past example was Fairfax Financial Holdings buying, through its investee company Thomas Cook, a majority stake in Quess Corp before it was listed. This signalled the bullish growth prospects of outsourcing of non-core activities by corporates.

Some of the favourite sectors of private players between 2013 and 2019 are:

- consumer (quick service restaurants, dairy, food, building materials, home furnishings);
- financial services (housing finance; microfinancing; fintech),
- healthcare (insurance, hospitals, pharma);
- B2B businesses (services companies, specialty chemicals, logistics, high-tech or precision engineering, technology, auto components and others).

It is noteworthy that private equity players generally do not invest in commodity or capex-heavy slow growth businesses. The above list of sectors is a long list of hunting grounds for investors. These sectors are benefitting from the mega trend of rising consumerism and urbanization. These two themes should continue in India for at least a decade, if not longer.

8

BLACK HERON'S UMBRELLA—
UNIQUELY DESIGNED TO COMPETE

Business is war. I go out there, I want to kill the competitors. I want to make their lives miserable. I want to steal their market share. I want them to fear me and I want everyone on my team thinking we're going to win.

—Kevin O'Leary, Canadian
businessman and TV personality

We witnessed an act that was designed to kill while on a safari at Lake Manyara National Park, Tanzania. We spotted a lone black heron, named after its black coloured plumage, in its hunting territory in the shallow Lake Manyara. Here little fishes hide in the dark areas of vegetation. The heron has devised a specialized strategy to trap and catch these fishes. It walks through the shallows, agitating the water. After a few steps, it lowers its head and spreads its wings up and forward—to form a dome-shaped canopy (or an umbrella), over its lowered head. Then it crouches down until the umbrella is almost touching the surface. This effectively turns the area dark. This pose serves two purposes. One, it creates shade, allowing the bird to see through the water by reducing the sun's glare. Two, it attracts fishes. The fishes that were scattered by the agitated water come and take refuge under the canopy-trap, thinking it to be one of the darker areas of vegetation. Upon seeing a fish, the heron quickly nudges its beak under the water's surface to pull out a wriggling fish, and finally swallows the catch. This is a very effective and efficient process.

We observed an equally fascinating act which was designed to kill while walking along the one-mile loop boardwalk of the Pitcher Plant Trail at the Big Thicket National Preserve in Texas. There my family and I enjoyed the sight of a large bog of pitcher plants. Each plant has a deep cavity, resembling a trumpet filled with liquid at the bottom. The cupped and widely protruding opening of the trumpet releases fragrant nectar to entice insects. The insect upon coming into contact with the opening, slips on the smooth surface and falls directly into the bottom liquid of the trumpet. The waxy scales and downward-facing hairs of the cavity make escape impossible. After some struggle, the prey drowns. The plant discharges a digestive acid that extracts the nutrients from the dead insect. The pitcher's trap is effective and foolproof. Some of the larger pitcher plants can even catch preys as big as a rat.

SWEET SPOT

Charlie Munger said, 'In nature and in business, specialization is key. Just as in an ecosystem, people who narrowly specialize can get good at occupying some little niche. *Just as animals flourish in niches, similarly, people specialize in the business world*—and get very good because they specialize—frequently find good economics that they wouldn't get any other way.'

Specialization and finding your niche are useful both in the animal kingdom and the corporate world. In the case of the black heron, its ability to make an umbrella out of its wings is the key factor that helps it to create its niche hunting style. Herons employ no other strategy but that of an umbrella trap to catch their prey. It works, so why should they stray? Moreover, animals are not greedy. Their needs are limited to the food they can eat promptly. They do not hoard or trade their catch. This characteristic keeps them bound to their niche territory.

Coming to the business world, one way a business develops its niche is by serving the existing specialized market that is ignored by basic or leading enterprises. The niche player enjoys superior economics initially. As the niche entity grows, it may attract some competition. But, it stays ahead of the game either due to its first mover advantage or due to unique features of the business. In the case of the Government Employees Insurance Company (GEICO), the insurance arm of Berkshire Hathaway, it had both the benefits. It was the first company to adopt a direct marketing approach. This approach helped it keep its costs low, to pass the cost savings to customers and gain scale. The scale allowed it to build the brand. The branding and low cost became a USP that allowed it to stay ahead of the competition.

Interestingly, the purple-throated carib, a type of hummingbird found in the Antillean Islands in the Caribbean, has a heaven-made match between itself and the flowering heliconia plants it feeds on. They both have adapted various traits which make them suitable for each other, thus negating any competition. For example, the heliconia plant relies on the Carib bird for pollination and provides sucrose-rich nectar, which the Caribs like and the competitor insects hate. For investors, state-owned NBCC (India) Ltd, formerly known as the National Buildings Construction Cooperation Ltd (NBCC) is the carib bird that feeds on government contracts for real estate and infrastructure development (the heliconia plant in this scenario). The NBCC receives these contracts through nomination by the ministries, and are precluded from competitive bidding (much like other insects who don't get the nectar). In 2012, the NBCC had more cash than its market capitalization and since then it has risen more than fifteen times. This happened gradually as investors realized its attractive business model, strong balance sheet, negative working capital, and strong and growing order book.

A scientist who studied the Carib-heliconia relationship proclaimed it to be the most convincing evidence for coevolution that they have ever seen. Similarly, in the past, Indian markets have seen many such hummingbirds: some examples are Polaris Financial Technology (one of the first vendors to the Citi Group), RS Software (India) Ltd (provided payment processing to Visa Inc.) and Balaji Telefilms (produced TV serials for Star India). Unfortunately, all these relationships ended in a divorce. What was missing? The match was not a long-lasting one to start with. It was too commercial, and most commercial bonds eventually end. Will the NBCC contract with the government meet the same fate? It is not purely commercial, and so has a much higher chance of survival.

INTELLIGENT FANATICS

I am borrowing the title and the content of this section from my B-school Professor, Sanjay Bakshi's mid-2015 talk that highlighted that a corporate is designed to kill (that is, generate superior returns) if run by 'intelligent fanatics'. Intelligent fanatics display three qualities: focus, integrity and intelligence. Quoting Charlie Munger again, 'If you get an opportunity to get into a wonderful business that's being run by an intelligent fanatic and if you don't load up, it's a big mistake.'

In the talk, Professor Bakshi described a few corporations with intelligent fanatics behind them. First is Eicher Motors' (EICHERMOT) Siddhartha Lal, who is crazy about touring bikes. His passion turned the near bankrupt Royal Enfield (owned by EICHERMOT) into a business with Rs 470 billion market capitalization—yes, literally a phoenix rising from the ashes. Royal Enfield has been making the iconic bullet bikes for ninety years but has remained a loss-making unit. After seven years of restructuring, Royal Enfield sold more bikes than Harley Davidson and turned very profitable. It generated pre-tax RoE of 58 per cent with no debt. Between 2010 and 2019, the EICHERMOT stock rose by twenty times.

Second on the list is Relaxo Footwear's (RELAXO) founder, Ramesh Dua. RELAXO makes good-quality, affordable branded footwear for India's masses, just like Havaianas did for Brazilians thirty years ago. RELAXO annually sells 120 million plus pairs of footwear for less than US$ 2/pair (Havaianas cheapest pair would cost US$ 18/pair) and made RoE of 32 per cent with minimal debt. Endorsed by popular movie stars, the company has become a prime example of buying commodities and converting them into branded products and selling them at lucrative profits.

Third on the list is Achal Bakeri. He runs the world's largest air cooler company, called Symphony Ltd. (SYMPHONY). He runs an asset-light company with its manufacturing part of the value chain outsourced. This keeps R&D, branding, marketing and distribution in-house. His focus is to become the dominant air cooler company globally and in every market wherever there is heat, low humidity and a middle class that cannot afford an air conditioner. SYMPHONY is debt free and earned the RoE of 90 per cent (adjusted for cash in the books) with very fast growth.

Fourth on the list is Quess Corp's (QUESS) founder Ajit Isaac. QUESS is the leader in business service outsourcing in

India. It started as a manpower outsourcing company in 2007, and inorganically acquired various adjacent business service outsourcing companies. Its revenues grew from Rs 2.7 billion in 2011 to Rs 85 billion in 2019. Ajit's focus is to make the client's non-core but critical functions, QUESS's core function, and deliver them—echoing his philosophy that 'No work is too small'. QUESS was listed in bourses in July 2016.

Last on the list is Sandeep Engineer. His company Astral Polytechnic (ASTRAL) makes plumbing pipes using resin acquired from Lubrizol—a Berkshire Hathaway company. These boring B2B plumbing products are his focus, and to add some flavour he has converted them into an iconic consumer brand though clever product placement in movies and by hiring a brand ambassador. The stock increased by forty times between mid-2010 and early 2019.

As made explicit in the above, these founders have a laserlike focus on their businesses. Their integrity is equally envious, if not more. In 2008, Siddhartha Lal began a joint venture with Volvo, which required him to sell 13 per cent of his stakes in the business to Volvo. The transaction took place at Rs 691/share when the market price was Rs 200/share. Siddhartha Lal structured the transaction so that minority shareholders could offload 13 per cent of their holding at the same price that he had received. Similarly, Ramesh Dua owned the footwear brand in his personal capacity. He transferred the brand to the company for virtually nothing. Alternatively, he could have decided to enjoy royalties at the expense of the minority shareholder. But he didn't.

Lastly, they are intelligent. By intelligence we are referring simply to these fanatics not doing dumb things. The four dumb things an entrepreneur can do are:

1. overaggression—manifests as excessive leverage;
2. growth without paying attention to profitability;

3. a penchant for gambling;
4. aversion to delegate, thereby limiting growth.

None of these vices are present in the above fanatics. To the contrary, these fanatics are low-profile, frugal and conservative. Most of them have no debt and they have strong balance sheets. They run profitable businesses. And most of them have delivered growth without equity dilution. They are not control freaks and seek professional help. For instance, Siddhartha Lal hired a marketing expert from Unilever, a business development expert from Harley Davidson and the head of motorbikes design for Ducati. All of them are intelligent fanatics in the true sense of the term.

Apart from being intelligent fanatics, guess what is the common theme across all their businesses? Do give a bit of hard thinking before continuing to read.

Peter Thiel in his book *Zero to One* wrote, 'The next Bill Gates will not build an operating system. The next Larry Page or Sergey Brin won't make a search engine. And the next Mark Zuckerberg won't create a social network. If you are copying these guys, you aren't learning from them. Of course, it's easier to copy a model than to make something new. Doing what we already know how to do takes the world from 1 to n, adding more of something familiar. But every time we create something new, we go from 0 to 1. The act of creation is singular, as is the moment of creation, and the result is something fresh and strange.'

Our intelligent fanatics did not necessarily create something new, but they unsuspectingly pulled their gold nuggets straight out of the dirt, a 0 to 1 act:

1. Siddhartha Lal from a bankrupt legacy business;

2. Ramesh Dua built on the niche of flip-flops, not formal or casual footwear;
3. Achal Bakeri focused on air coolers, not air conditioners;
4. Ajit from providing non-core basic business services, not consulting, R&D or executive hiring; and
5. Sandeep Engineer built on boring plumbing pipes, not classy kitchen or bathroom fittings.

They all build successful brands from products which were not brandworthy to start with. It requires changing customer perception as well as creating a new market that does not necessarily exist. They are as intelligent as they are fanatics—true wealth creators.

THE HOUSE ALWAYS WINS

Siddhartha Lal showed that one's passion could do wonders for an entrepreneur. He is a passionate biker. So is Jaydev Mody, a passionate gambling and horse racing enthusiast. He learned that the casino house always wins. Similar to Heron's umbrella wings which are perfectly designed to kill the prey, odds of every game and slot machine are always in favour of the casino to win. He thus turned into an entrepreneur within the space. Jaydev Mody runs the only listed gaming company in the Indian bourses—Delta Corp Ltd (DELTACORP). DELTACORP has established its leadership in the gaming space by owning roughly 1,800 gaming positions, spread across a few gaming facilities in the state of Goa. Additionally, it has an integrated casino resort in Daman, with 1,200 gaming positions awaiting regulatory approval.

Prior to this, Jaydev Mody was into realty and textiles. Around 2006, when the Piramal group of companies split, he was faced with a choice of working with either his sister, Urvi Piramal, or his friend Ajay Piramal (brother of Urvi's deceased husband)—Jaydev

Mody instead decided to retire at fifty and spend some more time with his wife and distinguished corporate lawyer, Zia Mody, and their three daughters.

India's gaming casino market is underpenetrated; given its paltry size of approximately US$ 150 million (in 2019) as compared to the global size of it at US$ 183 billion, which raises the possibility of huge growth potential. Growth in the global gaming industry comes primarily from the Asia—Pacific region (Singapore and Macau), which now has a 45 per cent global share. This serves to highlight the gambling propensity of Asians. Indians gamble mostly through unorganized and illegal channels. For example, in a World Cup cricket match, more than US$ 1.5 billion bets are from India. The most important thing is industry economics. This market is a high-operating leverage play. Initially, the set-up costs are high, but once a certain scale is reached, then the cash counter will not stop ringing. This will result in high margin and RoE play.

Jaydev Mody exited DELTACORP's heavy real estate assets in 2014 and shifted his focus to the gaming segment, as real estate did not provide the kind of return on capital which gaming could. DELTACORP raised its advertising spending to 4 per cent of sales to attract customers. Daman's casino resort opened in 2014 and till mid-2019 has been waiting for regulatory approval to operate the casino, which would have increased Delta's total gaming positions by almost 65 per cent. This will be Daman's first casino and it is strategically located to tap 35 million population within a 350-km radius.

In the fiscal year 2015, DELTACORP's revenue was Rs 3 billion and its EBITDA margin was 22 per cent. This is low for a gaming company and is due to low utilization of the gaming position of around 60 per cent. In the next four years, revenue could jump 50 per cent and the EBITDA margin could rise to 35 per cent, without accounting for contributions from Daman's casino as regulatory approvals remained uncertain. Against this, the company was available at a market capitalization of Rs 20 billion and enterprise value of Rs 23 billion.

Jaydev Mody's passion and background, DELTACORP's leadership position in a nascent industry with significant growth prospects and lastly, the economics of the gaming industry attracted me to the stock. Rakesh Jhunjhunwala held 5 per cent plus in the stock and that only added to my comfort.

After my purchases, a few positive things happened. DELTACORP acquired an online gaming site, adda52.com. This and improvements in the Goa casinos' revenue collection pushed revenue by the fiscal year 2019 to Rs 8 billion[1] and EBITDA margin to 40 per cent. Receiving approval to open the Daman casino can be the next trigger for the stock. On the negative side, the casinos in India are subject to heavy regulatory and tax overhang. In mid-2019, the stock price was under pressure as it was speculated that the company might be subject to 28 per cent Goods and Services Tax (GST) on all the bets waged and not on the casino's revenues. Jury is still out there but a 28 per cent tax on the total amount bet will kill the casino industry, and so tax relief is expected.

STAR CEMENT (STARCEMENT)

Star Cement Ltd (STARCEMENT) is the largest cement manufacturer in the northeastern region (NER) of India with a regional market share of 23 per cent. STARCEMENT, along with their two close competitors, control 72 per cent of NER's total cement capacity. Like black herons' umbrella, STARCEMENT regional location was designed to kill competition.

NER is mostly a landlocked, hilly region in India that is geographically isolated and inaccessible. STARCEMENT's manufacturing plants (cement clinker and grinding units) have easy access to customers in the NER market, standing at a distance of only 285 km as compared to the 1,000 km for its competitors that are located outside the NER. The location proximity gives the company a significant advantage, due to the high transportation costs of moving bulky cement.

In terms of manufacturing costs, limestone and power account for 40-45 per cent of the total. STARCEMENT has control over these costs via its captive power plant and its limestone mine. Its mine is one of the best in terms of quality in India, with a calcium oxide content of 49 per cent as compared to the pan-India average of 42 per cent. Its limestone mine is within 2-3 km from the clinker plant, and the reserves are sufficient to meet its needs for the next hundred years. STARCEMENT's coal-based power plant results in cost savings vs buying off the grid; it also provides an uninterrupted supply. The coal plant is located 10-20 km from the coalfields of Coal India Ltd, ensuring low raw material transportation costs.

STARCEMENT's 870 exclusive dealers are spread across the region, including deep into the retail segment in rural areas. Fuelled by the strong brand, its retail network is 25 per cent larger than its nearest competitor and peer, Dalmia Bharat Sugar and Industries Ltd (DALMIASUG). Its retail segment contributes 83 per cent of sales as compared to the 50 per cent for DALMIASUG. The strong brand and its retail concentration allow it to realize 10-15 per cent higher prices than the industrial/infrastructure segment.

The above dynamics result in industry-leading financials for STARCEMENT with EBITDA per tonne at around Rs 1700 plus/tonne vs Rs 900/tonne for its peers. Strong profitability has allowed it to expand its cement-grinding capacity by 9 times in the last thirteen years. STARCEMENT capacity in 2019 was 4.3 mtpa and intends to increase it to 10 mtpa by 2022.[2] The expansion is to come from the eastern region, outside of the NER, allowing it to diversify its revenue. A strong balance sheet and falling debt means that most of it can be funded internally.

With the infrastructure poor, NER has per capita cement consumption only at 131 kg per person, the lowest in India. The government is pushing for housing, roads, airports, railway networks and smart cities located in the NER and that should push the cement demand growth to 8-9 per cent (vs 6 per cent CAGR for the last five years). Despite the expected rise in demand, a limited capacity addition has been announced in the NER due to unfavourable regulation, relating to mining licences and environmental clearances. Rising growth prospects and limited additions mean that the market leader STARCEMENT and the incumbent players should continue to benefit.

CONGLOMERATED NICHE

BPL Ltd. (BPL), a victim of liberalization and the fallen electronics giant, is making a comeback. All it has is its brand name. It lacks a distribution set-up as well as a manufacturing unit. It sources its parts from China and assembles it in-house. It then sells them online through Amazon. Amrutanjan Health Care (AMRUTANJAN) is another example that comes to mind. It is also leveraging e-tailing.

Access to markets has become easier than ever before, allowing niche and small companies to experiment and give birth to niche products which otherwise would have never seen the light of the day.

In the book *The Long Tail*, Chris Anderson, argues that niche products which are in low demand or have low sales volume, can in aggregation build a better market share than an individual bestseller and blockbuster—if the dissemination channel is wide enough. In essence, he is referring to casting the net wide enough to be able to catch most of the fish that are sparsely spread over a very large territory. The internet allows you to do just that, providing reach which is otherwise inconceivable. From this lens, YouTube, Amazon, Flipkart and Netflix are providing a great service to niche products and services. These organizations have become conglomerated niches themselves. YouTube, for instance, aggregates and then provides to its users all kinds of videos, without differentiating between blockbusters and niche videos. Baba Sehgal, the first Hindi rap megastar is taking full advantage of it. Most of his videos have a couple of hundred thousand views already. On the other end of the spectrum, you have Lilly Singh's funny videos and Vidya Vox's music videos. Some of their videos have even clocked 10 plus million views. Suddenly, niche videos are breathing a life of their own through YouTube.

Amazon and Flipkart too are aggregating vendors for products ranging from large electronic items to numerous niche products such as textile 'products crafted by women', serving the mission of women empowerment. Netflix has 125 million plus subscribers binging on niche content (such as *Marseille*, a French political drama; or *Hibana*, a Japanese drama; or *Sacred Games*, a Hindi crime thriller). It is synonymous to an expansive library with many floors where each of those floors has multiple rooms. Most subscribers never visit all the floors. Instead, they stay in corners that match their tastes. But by providing blockbusters as well as niche categories, these technology biggies have become a one-stop solution for both niche sellers and users. This is the argument Chris Anderson is making. By aggregating these niches, the cumulative sales will be bigger than any blockbuster individually. The internet allows this aggregation economically; thereby benefiting niche sellers and users at the expense of blockbusters.

Flipkart's revenues for instance reached US$ 4.3 billion in the fiscal year 2018. Niche products should have almost reached US$ 1.3 billion in sales, assuming 30 per cent share of the total sales as observed in the case of Amazon, Netflix and Rhapsody. Flipkart's niche category in aggregate, dwarfs all the established retail brands in the country except Tanishq (jewellery sales at approximately US$ 2.3 billion[3]) and ITC (cigarette sales at US$ 3.2 billion[4] plus). All the other single blockbuster retail brands owned by Raymond, Nestle and Unilever are big but not huge enough for example, Surf Excel is one of the biggest brands of Unilever but its sales is close to US$ 0.5 billion.

9

HACHI DOG—CONSISTENTLY LOYAL TO HIS OWNER

I pray to be like the ocean, with soft currents, maybe waves at time. More and more, I want the consistency rather than the highs and lows.

—Drew Barrymore, American actress,
author and entrepreneur

In 1924, Hidesaburo Ueno, a professor in the University of Tokyo, took Hachikō (referred here by his more popular name Hachi based on the Hollywood movie discussed later in the chapter), a golden brown Akita breed puppy as pet. Every evening, Hachi would leave his home to greet Ueno at the nearby Shibuya Station, where they parted ways in the morning as Ueno would commute to work. This continued every single day until May 1925, when one evening, Ueno did not return. He died of cerebral haemorrhage while he had been giving a lecture. Hachi continued to perform his daily routine, appearing at the station awaiting Ueno's return.

The initial reaction of passers-by, including the people who knew Uneo was not friendly—they failed to understand his emotion and intent. Nevertheless, this did not deter Hachi from his daily routine and he patiently waited every day.

However, things took a different turn in 1932. Hirokichi Saito, Ueno's student, learned extensively about the Akita breed, and as part of his research, studied the history of Hachi's life. He published a documented census of the Akita breed in Japan, stating that only thirty pure-bred Akitas were still alive, which included Hachi. He would frequent Shibuya Station to visit Hachi, and published several articles about the dog's remarkable loyalty. Hachi highlighted the 'strong bond with family' characteristics of the Akita breed. These articles started to benefit Hachi. The new-found popularity ensured real benefits—food, as he waited for his Ueno. Hachi continued his daily routine for the next nine years, nine months and fifteen days, after which Hachi died. Only death stopped him from waiting!

Hachi drew national attention: a renowned artist carved his sculpture, the awareness of the Akita breed grew and his legendary faithfulness became a national symbol of loyalty. More recently, Richard Gere starred in a movie titled, *Hachi: A Dog's Tale* which was aired in 2009. It was a remake of the 1987 Japanese film, *Hachikō Monogatari*, literally translated as The Tale of Hachiko.

Hachi's is not a lone incident and similar such incidents portraying a dog's loyalty have been noted in other parts of the world in films like *Greyfriars Bobby*, about a Skye Terrier of Edinburgh; *Old Shep*, about a sheep dog in Montana, the US; *Kostya* about a German Shepherd of Tolyatti, Russia. Each of these dogs had spent years waiting for the master at a particular spot, after their master's death. And like Hachi, these dogs have died waiting and have not strayed—even for a single day.

HOW TO SPOT A HACHI IN THE INVESTMENT JUNGLE?

Dogs are loyal. Nevertheless, Hachi's loyalty was unimaginable. An investor's dream is to own stocks that are equivalent to Hachi (let us call them Hachi stocks). Such stocks are loyal to the owner and reward them with strong returns year after year. In earlier chapters, uncertainty or cyclical distress, or some kind of trigger or even special competitive advantage were the key reasons behind returns. Timing one's entry is essential in these cases. But Hachi stocks, to the contrary, compound returns consistently year after year, thereby reducing the importance of the timing of entry and exit. Total returns are correlated more to the length of the holding period rather than to the entry/exit timing. The longer the hold, greater the absolute returns.

But, the key question is, what makes a stock a Hachi stock?

It is consistent performance which results in trustworthy loyalty. This happens when a stock produces profitable growth, year after year. To find Hachi stocks, I started screening some 5,000 listed Indian companies. I took fifteen years as my observation period. Fifteen years is a long time to judge loyalty. During this period, a company has to exhibit consistent profitable growth, that is, achieve a 10 per cent revenue growth annually (without excessive equity dilution or leverage), while earning 15 per cent RoE. India's nominal GDP growth for the last ten years, and since 1990, has averaged 14 per cent. Therefore, 14 per cent looks like a reasonable revenue growth that we should expect. But there are very few companies who could consistently clock 14 per cent revenue growth. So I considered 10 per cent as a compromise to suit the reality in this case. Roughly, 25 per cent to 30 per cent of the entire listings have achieved the RoE of 15 per cent or more, and very few companies have consistently been able to achieve 20 per cent. Therefore, I took the RoE of 15 per cent as the unexpected minimum. We can also calculate India's cost of equity by adding India's risk-free rate and equity risk premium. India's risk-free rate is the ten-year sovereign bond yield and it has moved around 7.5 per cent in the last 10 to 15 years. The Indian equity risk premium is almost 8 per cent calculated by adding the US's equity risk premium of approximately 5 per cent to India's credit default spread, which is around 3 per cent. Adding both, we get India's cost of equity of roughly 15.5 per cent—making the RoE of 15 per cent a reasonable expectation. Additionally, the 2017 survey by E&Y showed that the listed Indian companies' cost of equity is around 15 per cent.[1]

Just to clarify, we are looking for companies that achieve 10 per cent revenue growth every single year during this fifteen-year period. This is different from achieving a 10 per cent compounded average growth rate. Consistent growth every year, as opposed to compounded growth rate, exhibits excellence—as it shows growth under all circumstances and during all phases of an economic and sector cycle. It also reduces nasty surprises and projects certainty—something the market celebrates. Also you may ask, why have I not considered the growth of net profit or earnings per share (EPS) rather than RoE? This is because the net profit and EPS are heavily influenced by the company's cost structure and commodity raw material costs, which mostly are mean reverting. Due to their mean reverting nature, the EPS does not always show a nice growth trajectory like revenue. And so EPS fails to convey the true picture of the business when compared on a yearly basis. One may argue that dividend-paying stocks are truly Hachi stocks. Though this may not always be the case. Dividend is discretionary, it does not reflect the business fundamentals and can be paid though borrowings as well.

Screening output: I screened the data of the last fifteen (2004-19) of all the listed Indian companies.[2] It was remarkable to observe that in any random year, around 25-35 per cent companies secured

10 per cent revenue growth, and almost 30-35 per cent companies generated 15 per cent RoE. Clearly, we have set a low bar. But the challenge was for a company to cross both the revenue and RoE parameters for fifteen consecutive years. Any guesses as to how many could do so consistently?

Only four could do it every single year for the last fifteen years (2004-19). Any guesses as to who they are?

They are HDFC Bank, Page Industries, Astral Poly Technik and Muthoot Capital Services. The Hachi stocks! I checked as far back as I could go in history, and these companies consistently met our criteria. The consistency of these four companies' historical financials beat 99.9 per cent of the listed Indian corporations. It is quite a feat. I have to mention that in the fiscal year 2018, Astral Poly Technik's revenue growth did not meet the cut, but its RoE remained above 15 per cent and therefore, I made an exception and included it in my list.

Of the three above-mentioned criteria, a duration of fifteen years was the most demanding and that is where most companies faltered. So out of curiosity, I shortened the duration to ten years. Now, thirty-one companies (approximately 1 per cent of the universe) were able to meet our criteria, that is, reaching our revenue and RoE levels for each of the ten consecutive years during 2009-19.

My observations are as follows:

- Apollo Hospitals Enterprise has grown its revenues significantly more than 10 per cent for every single year during the last fifteen years. The challenge was that Apollo's RoEs have consistently stayed below 15 per cent due to heavy capital expenditure.
- Asian Paints and Berger Paints have met all our criteria since 2003. Except that in the fiscal years 2016 and 2017, both companies' revenue fell below 10 per cent.

- Motherson Sumi Systems have met all our criteria since 2003. However, the Volkswagen fiasco, pushed the revenue growth below 10 per cent in the fiscal year 2016.
- Technology and telecom companies have met out criteria till 2011/2012. Since then, and especially in the more recent years, they have been seeing weak revenue growth due to sector-specific challenges.

It is easy to reach the top but very tough to remain there. What we can derive the most comfort from among the four Hachi stocks we have found is that each of them have belonged to different sectors. This means that none of them is benefiting from a sector tailwind and that they are Hachi stocks because of their special characteristics, namely: laser focus, ethical management and prudent capital allocation. Additionally, the four stocks should continue to stay on top, as there is still significant room to grow. HDFC Bank will benefit from the public sector bank's misery (public sector banks are still 70 per cent of India's banking system). Page Industries has significant room to grow in the country with very favourable demographics and growing income levels. Astra Poly Technik will continue to replace plumbing lead pipes—as the majority of them are still made of lead—by chlorinated polyvinyl chloride (CPVC) pipes. Muthoot Capital Services, even after their stellar past growth, only has a market capitalization of approximately Rs 15 billion and has significant cross-selling, new products and new geographic opportunities.

A caveat—this exercise excludes companies listed in the last few years for which data for the last 10 to 15 years are not available.

Saurabh Mukherjea dedicated his book, *The Unusual Billionaires* to this theme. In the book, he identified eight companies that are ideally suited for a buy and hold strategy. The companies identified are Asian Paints, Astral Poly Technik, Berger Paints, ITC, Marico,

Page Industries, HDFC Bank and Axis Bank. He identified these companies in April 2016. His criteria was 10 per cent revenue growth and 10 per cent RoE for a consecutive ten-year period. His criteria is almost similar to what I have used to identify Hachi stocks. One notable difference is that, while my criteria looks back for fifteen years, he considered ten years. But my criteria only filtered out HDFC Bank, Astral Poly Technik and Page Industries of the above eight companies. This is because all the other remaining companies saw their revenue growth fall below the 10 per cent threshold in the fiscal year 2016 and/or 2017.

ASTRAL POLY TECHNIK (ASTRAL)

Astral Poly Technik (ASTRAL) provides a testimony to the fact that any product consumed by an end-consumer can be branded. It all started in March 1996, when Sandeep Engineer incorporated ASTRAL, armed with technical know-how from Lubrizol (the US) and joint venture with Thomson Plastics (the US) to produce CPVC pipes that were to be used for industrial transportation and plumbing. Back then, pipes were made of metals which made them prone to corrosion, leading to leakages and damp conditions. Convinced of the quality of the product, Engineer targeted industrial clients to sell his plastic pipes to and received very tepid responses. Capacity utilization was close to zilch and his main banker collapsed, pushing ASTRAL very close to bankruptcy.

With financial support from Thomson Plastics, Engineer averted this crisis. And, on Lubrizol's suggestion, he shifted his focus to the residential plumbing segment which was easier than competing with established players in the industrial segment. With some challenges, he was able to woo a few real estate developers and hotels to use CPVC pipes for their plumbing needs. The real breakthrough came when he lowered the price of his CPVC pipes, to match the conventional galvanized iron (GI) pipes, even though it meant that he would bear some losses initially. He would have and did make up for the loss by charging a premium on the fitting services. Additionally, he realized that plumbers, not customers, are the influencers. He started wooing the plumbers. By lowering the sales price, wooing the right decision-makers and an innovative branding of mundane plumbing pipes turned the tide for him. He thus created a market and then focused on expanding production capacity to reap the benefits of his efforts. For instance, ASTRAL expanded capacity by 15 times since 2007.[3] He maintained his focus on marketing and branding, making CPVC pipes synonymous with ASTRAL pipes. All this deepened ASTRAL's competitive advantage, increased its brand value and lowered working capital needs. Listed in April 2007, by May 2019, ASTRAL's share prices rose almost 120 times (Rs 140 billion in May 2019) and revenues during this time rose to about twenty-four times.

ASTRAL's recipes for success are manifold. But they all boil down to a few things:

Management: The conviction and focus of Engineer led him to overcome all the hurdles; his willingness to delegate key functions to the right candidates.

Product: The tie-up with Lubrizol enabled ASTRAL to produce high-quality products and launch innovative products frequently.

Production: Pan-India manufacturing was set up and it had the largest capacity in India.

Marketing: Strong relationships with distributions and plumbers were built over the years.

Capital: A prudent capital allocation.

PAGE INDUSTRY (PAGEIND)

Empowered by the licensee of the Jockey brand of innerwear, Page Industry (PAGEIND) had a phenomenal run since its March 2007 listing. Share prices increased by sixty-four times (Rs 219 billion in May 2019) and revenues went up by twenty-three times until March 2019.[4] Various successful American garment brands entered India in the last two decades or so. Most of these brands are housed under two well-regarded companies: Arvind Fashions Ltd (ARVINDFASN) and Aditya Birla Fashion and Retail Ltd (ABFRL). In 2019, Page's market capitalization has surpassed the combined market capitalization of both these companies. PAGEIND is a rare success story which has been handcrafted by Sunder Genomal, the promoter. Many variables have had to come together to weave such a success.

Brand: The presence of a brand is not enough. Sunder, through innovative media and in-store advertisements, converted it into an aspirational brand. PAGEIND regularly spends 5 per cent of its annual revenue on advertisements. 'Just Jockeying' and 'Jockey or nothing' were brands campaigns which cast the magic. To keep the brand value intact, Jockey differentiates itself from the other brands by having a strict pricing discipline, which prohibits its retailers from selling below the maximum retail price (MRP).

Quality product: Jockey innerwear are high-quality, desirable products that are backed by consistent innovation and frequent launches. New products are launched every three months and slow-moving products are removed from the retailers' inventory. Beyond men's innerwear, Jockey has also launched products for women and leisure wear. Given its brand image, over time it can launch products in many other categories to tap the full market potential.

Production: To maintain the quality and a prompt supply of products to distributors, PAGEIND keeps manufacturing in-house. But this is a catch-22 situation as it is a labour-intensive industry and raises risks of labour unrest. PAGEIND has cracked it through cordial relationship. PAGEIND introduced free lunches in late 2000s, which was eventually adopted by the industry. The company mostly hires women and younger labour with limited experience. Additionally, production sites are spread across geographically dispersed multiple facilities, thereby significantly reducing chances of a union and strikes. The right work environment and adequate training has reduced worker attrition to one of the lowest in the industry. Managing labour relations is the key in this industry. For instance, in the fiscal year 2002, Jockey's competitors TTK Tantex and Associated Apparels suffered labour strikes, which led to their exit from the industry.

Distribution: PAGEIND has 500 plus distributors (140 in the fiscal year 2007) catering to 50,000 retail outlets and points of sale. The Jockey product reaches customers through online channels, mom and pop shops, exclusive Jockey shops as well as large format anchor stores in shopping malls such as Shoppers Stop.

All of the above, prudent capital allocation and relentless focus on the brand has continued to deepen Jockey's competitive advantage and made it an aspirational brand with a strong demand-pull. All this is amply reflected in its financials as well. Its net profit margin in the last decade has hovered around 12-13 per cent and RoE between 40 and 60 per cent.

MUTHOOT CAPITAL SERVICES (MUTHOOTCAP)

The smallest company on this list, Muthoot Capital Services (MUTHOOTCAP) is a focused two-wheeler financier.

MUTHOOTCAP is not a market leader and faces competition from practically all the large banks. However, it enjoys sector tailwinds. India is the world's largest two-wheeler market selling around 50,000 plus units a day or about 20 million a year. The industry revenue is growing at high single to low tens annually. Only about 25-30 per cent of two-wheeler purchases are financed, compared to around 60 per cent for commercial vehicles. Thus, the two-wheeler lending industry is growing much faster than the overall industry at about 15-20 per cent, aided by rising financing penetration.

However, what has been working even better is its right parentage. Its parent, Muthoot Finance Ltd (MUTHOOTFIN) is a much larger and renowned gold financier with 4,325 branches in all Indian states and union territories. MUTHOOTCAP has been leveraging its parent's branches for a fee to cross-sell and mine existing customers whose credit history is already present with the parent company. This strategy has not only allowed MUTHOOTCAP an asset-light expansion, but also provided faster growth at a lower non-performing asset (NPA) rate compared to the self-acquired customers by MUTHOOTCAP. It is yet to tap some 50 per cent of its parent's branches.

MUTHOOTCAP's internal processes are robust.[5] They are all digitalized, leading to a fast and efficient lending process—mostly within a couple of hours. Their quick loan processing is critical in a two-wheeler financing business, where the customer would like to buy the vehicle expecting delivery on the same day. Its NPA remains low due to granular loan books, multilayered and robust collection team and its emphasis on lending for vehicles that are easier to resell in the case of a default.

MUTHOOTCAP is now expanding beyond the south and two-wheeler financing. It is venturing into the semi-urban markets of north and east India where competition from big banks is comparatively less. It has also launched used car finances and personal loans to better mine its existing and prospective customer base. Geographical and product diversification should lower the concentration risk and make the company more resilient.

I am skipping writing about HDFC Bank as much has already been written and whatever I will write here will be dwarfed by what is already out there.

After a lot of thinking to generalize what is common among all these four consistent performers, I realized that there could not be any secret sauce that is amenable to be copied in order to produce another such consistent performer, another Hachi stock. They have everything going right for them that is, sector tailwinds, exceptional management quality and flawless execution. However, one cannot discount the fact that in each of these examples there is an element of luck in the form of a first mover advantage, or simply by being at the right place at the right time.

10

BACTERIA'S EVOLUTION— UNSTOPPABLE INNOVATION

The second you get set in your ways is the second a newer, fresher, more innovative company is going to come in and take your market share.

—Rachel Hollis, American author

Scientists of Harvard Medical School and Technion-Israel Institute of Technology constructed a 2 by 4 foot petri dish.[1] The dish was divided into nine vertical bands, and the base of each band was filled with thick agar—a seaweed-derived, jellylike substance to nourish the bacterium *E. coli*. To observe how the bacteria would adapt to increasingly higher doses of antibiotics, scientists saturated the bands with varying doses of the same. The outermost bands were free of any drug. The next, inner bands, contained a small amount of antibiotic; say one dose—just above the minimum needed to kill the bacteria. Inside that band, the succeeding inner bands had ten doses of the drug. Proceeding further in, the subsequent bands had hundred doses of the drug.

Finally, we reach the middle band, containing 1,000 doses of the drug. Across the top of the bands, scientists poured thin agar to facilitate bacterial movement around the bands. The background is black, while the bacteria are white in colour.

Left undisturbed, the petri dish first developed a thick layer of white bacteria in the outermost bands that had no antibiotic, up until the point that they could no longer survive; then they hit the inner bands with the single antibiotic dose. Then a mutant appeared. It resisted the single antibiotic dose and started to spread—first gradually, and then at its usual pace once it developed full resistance. Then the other mutants, those that also developed a resistance, appeared and provided competition to the mutant that had first moved. When these mutants hit the next inner boundary of the band that has ten doses, they again had to pause and develop new mutations to be able to cross over. Then new mutants appear and this process was repeated in the bands having hundred antibiotic doses. After about eleven days, the bacteria finally made it to the middle band having 1,000 antibiotic doses. Through this process of accumulative, successive mutation, bacteria that are sensitive to antibiotics evolve to resist extremely high drug concentrations within a short period. The experiment displays unstoppable and continuous evolution.

The petri dish experiment also explains the evolution of countries, sectors and companies. Countries start in the outermost bands—when their per capita income is low, and they are what we know as an agrarian society. Then the economy diversifies and starts mining, basic manufacturing, construction, financial services, retail and so on. As they continue to evolve, they add other sophisticated sectors through innovation as well as advance their basic sectors to the next level. Most of the large, developed Western economies today have seen this progression over the years and are now inside or close to the middle band of the petri dish. There also remain countries that are still in the outermost bands and are yet to see the evolution of their economies. Prime examples are North Korea and a few countries in Sub-Saharan Africa. And then, there are all the emerging market countries, including India, which is somewhere between the outermost and the middle band of the dish. As the ongoing reforms provide the expected benefits and more reforms are put in place, India should gradually be nudged to move closer to the middle band over the coming years. Interestingly, some of the Gulf Cooperation Council (GCC) countries have almost jumped a band, that is, moved directly from a basic economy to a developed economy due to the availability of a significant amount of energy resources as compared to their domestic needs and their small population base. The absence of energy resources has in fact been a boon to some Asian countries, such as Japan, South Korea and Taiwan, all of who have focused on developing their high-technology sectors and exporting the products to pay for rising energy imports. These countries, consequently, have pushed their economies closer to or inside the middle band. Conversely, a few countries have reversed their movement and are now moving outwards due to civil wars. Recent examples of this are Syria and Venezuela.

Zooming into sectors—the petri dish, from its outer bands to the middle band can be represented as a generalized sector value chain. In a sector value chain, there are more number of bands. Nevertheless, conceptually, the comparison with this petri dish experiment holds. If we were to generalize, outer bands are a segment of the value chain or are subsectors with a lower entry barrier and conducive operating environment. The subsequent inner bands have significantly higher entry barriers due to a tougher operating environment. Consequently, outer bands face higher competition, lower growth and weaker financials when compared to the inner bands. If we were to look at the Indian information technology sector, it is possible that Tata Consultancy Services (TCS) is inside or close to the middle band, and a plethora of other small technology companies are closer to the outer bands.

Each band represents the market size of that segment. When companies in a band have fully tapped into its current market, they may consider exporting their goods and services to similar value chain segments (bands) of other countries or move into a new sector, that is, an entirely new petri dish. Another option is to move into a higher value chain (the inner bands) of their current sector (petri dish) using innovation (mutation). Even if a company is the first to innovate (mutate), and moves into the inner bands, it will not be the only one to do so for long. Eventually other innovators (mutants) will appear and compete for resources with the incumbent mutant. Thus, without regulation it is rare to have a monopoly in any particular band for a sustainable period. There is always competition.

In the above petri dish, it was notable to see that the mutant bacterium which had crossed over to the inner band was not necessarily the strongest, but only the closest to that very next band. The strongest were left behind many times; highlighting the importance of first mover advantage and of being in the right place, at the right time. A point of difference—in the corporate world first mover disadvantage is also common, something not observed in the petri dish.

Another parallel is that as the mutant breaks into the next band, initially its growth is slow, as it is still developing a resistance. Once it is fully resistant, it resumes normal growth. Similarly, as innovators move into higher value chain segments, initially the financials are weak. With a rising stronghold within the segment, revenue increases and the operating leverage kicks in, and the innovative companies start to see an improvement in their financials. We can also draw some parallels between a mutant bacterium in a new band to a start-up company that has disrupted the subsector (band). They have a significant untapped market to capture; not only in its current band but also over time in the other inner bands. Interestingly, these start-ups may not necessarily start from the outward most band, and need not cross each successive bands in order to reach the middle and the most coveted band. Most of the time, these start-ups arise directly in the middle band itself. Think of Uber, Airbnb and many others like them. Investors understand their potential and are happy to value these companies highly, even if they are loss making. For instance, Uber in its 2019 prospectus, ahead of a much-awaited IPO, imposingly asserted, 'Our mission is to ignite opportunity by setting the world in motion'. Though this is essentially vague and boastful, perhaps Uber here is referring to their ability to disrupt and capture the middle band of other sectors (petri dish) using their competitive edge in mobility or motion. As in the petri dish experiment, progress is built upon progress. Bacteria—with every mutation—becomes stronger and raises its ability to mutate again, even in a tougher environment. Similarly, with every innovation, innovator companies are strengthening their competitive advantage against their peers and building platforms for further innovation. I think that Uber's past strong revenue growth and its significant edge over its peers is their source of optimism. However, a word of caution may be adhered to here. The experiment of bacterial evolution teaches us that an inward movement is not assured for any mutant, and that competition can come from the least expected places.

Well, corporates don't always move inwards. Many corporates are standing still, while many are moving outwards. One of the recent examples is Valeant Pharmaceuticals (its name has been changed to Bausch Health Companies Inc.). Valeant, through a series of debt-fuelled aggressive acquisitions have ended up owning many highly regarded, patented drugs in its kitty. In its greed to boost its near-term profits, Valeant cut R&D expenditure of its recently acquired companies to zilch, employed accounting gimmicks and tax manoeuvres. It blatantly raised prices of the drugs it had acquired, including some life-saving and essential ones. The price rise was obnoxious enough to attract investigation by the US Senate House and the attorney offices. Subsequently, Valeant's share price fell by about 90 per cent. Valeant had a golden goose that it killed for its greed. The biggest lesson that the bacterial experiment can impart to corporates is to continuously innovate and move forward and avoid making stupid mistakes motivated by greed. Innovation is all the more important as their competitors are moving ahead wisely and business which do not innovate will have to fall behind.

If we were to generalize from the perspective of an investment style, outer bands are hunting grounds of value investors, while growth investors are expected to hunt inside or closer to the middle band. From the perspective of size, smaller companies are to be found in the outer bands and larger ones, closer to the middle bands. However, there are many exceptions to such a generalization.

The experiment also provides a few nuggets of wisdom. As higher antibiotic doses strengthen bacteria, similarly, tougher environments and hardships are the keys to growth and resilience. Constant smooth sailing does not always help in the end. Remember this the next time you are pampering your child. The experiment also highlights the phenomenon of an 'effect of effect'. Antibiotics have a temporary effect of stopping the bacteria with an unintended permanent consequence of strengthening what the antibiotics wanted to kill in the first place—bacteria.

11

GREEN HERON'S TRICK—PROMOTER BAITS INVESTORS

Wall Street never changes, the pockets change, the suckers change, the stocks change, but Wall Street never changes because human nature never changes.

—Jesse Livermore, American short seller

The green heron bird is common in north and central America. It has devised a shrewd trick to catch prey. It comes to the edge of a lake or a water body and drops bait, like a small piece of bread or a little fish on the water to attract bigger fish to the surface. Once it spots a big fish close to the surface approaching the floating bait, heron would with precision, dips its beak beneath the surface and in a fraction of a second, picks out the lured fish for its lunch. Well, herons are smart. Nevertheless, in the wild, even they are duped and become prey to more intelligent animals. Mugger crocodiles of India and American alligators are those intelligent animals. To catch herons, they cover their snouts with sticks and lay still for a long time just beneath the surface of the water. Perhaps they have learned that during their mating season, herons need sticks to build their nests. Attracted by the sticks, herons come close to pick them and in turn become a meal for the crocodiles and alligators. Similarly, in the shallow waters of East Africa, a species of cichlid fish sinks to the ground as if dead. It can spend up to fifteen minutes in this position, waiting in a still position. Smaller fish generally nibble on the cichlid corpse. As the small fish comes close enough, the cichlid fish snaps to life and nabs a meal (same strategies don't always work). Essentially, the hunter offers itself as a bait to attract prey.

Recollect that in Chapter 5, dolphins and whales would create uncertainty to lure fishes. A predator benefits from the prey's fearful disposition. On the contrary, in this chapter's examples, predators benefit from the preys' greedy nature. A prey is attracted towards easy lunch and comes too close to the predator. Consequently, a prey pays with its life. In equity markets, promoters often offer baits in terms of rosy guidance, galloping growth, lucrative stories and so on. Gullible investors, blinded by greed, take the financials and guidance at face value and fall for it. Hope of multibagger returns lure investors into the promoters' bait, and investors eventually lose a significant part of their principal. No wonder that there is a proverbial saying that greed and fear are the two worst sins of the stock market. This chapter focuses on protecting the principal rather than earning returns on it. In this sense, the chapter is more important than all the prior chapters combined.

Indian equities did not only gift multibaggers to investors. They also punished investors with value traps. Between January 2014 and mid-2019, almost one in every ten listed Indian companies lost more than 80 per cent of their value. Multiple reasons can be attributed to these wealth decimators:

MANAGEMENT

- Stealing/misleading shareholders
- Stories and hypes

BUSINESSES

- Weak balance sheet

OTHER PEOPLE'S MONEY

Unless a promoter is a saint, the desire to steal from minority shareholders is irresistible. The sense of fairness when dealing with other people's money is easily distorted. Still, many Indian promoters have dealt with the minority in an upright fashion. Various Indian companies are run by multidecades and even century-old renowned business families and they have a legacy at stake. Their rich legacy disincentivize them from exercising short-term hanky-panky tricks to fill their coffers at the expense of the minority. Moreover, they understand the long-term benefits of strong corporate governance on the company valuations and their ability to raise capital. In that sense, many promoters have matured.

Nevertheless, the risk of promoters stealing from the minority is very real. After every bull run, these treacherous promoters' tricks would come out in the open, leaving investors high and dry while they basked in the sunshine of their loot.

Of the recent examples, the most blatant is Company X's 'Pump and Dump' strategy (name withheld as the company has received a clean chit from the Securities and Exchange Board of

India [SEBI]). Anecdotal evidence is that Company X's promoter have been offering a fixed 24 per cent annual return to large investors in return for buying its stock from the open market. An old friend from school, and now a fund manager in Kolkata, was offered the same but he declined the offer. Rumour has it that this 24 per cent assured return scheme was in vogue from mid-2016 to late 2017 till the bull run in Indian equities lasted. Significant cornering of the shares through motivated purchases shrunk the free float and pushed share prices four times in eighteen months. Yes, the share price was also supported by stellar financials. Sales and net profit almost doubled during these eighteen months. While investors made off-market 24 per cent per annum in collusion with the promoter, the promoter himself kept all the remaining upside. All the dealings were off-market, leaving the promoter with significant profits mostly in black and in accounts not directly traceable to the promoter. From January 2018 onwards, its share price fell and its financials started to deteriorate significantly, suggesting convenient accounting window dressing while the promoter was riding the share prices up. Shortly thereafter, its share price fell 90 per cent and then its auditor resigned due to lack of adequate information provided by the company—like cops arriving at a crime scene after the damage is done.

Another interesting example is PC Jeweller Ltd. (PCJEWELLER). PCJEWELLER's promoter sold shares in the open market in multiple smaller tranches at near peak prices. Each of the tranche sizes was below reporting threshold to dodge reporting. Insider sales are negatively viewed by the markets. Once the market discovered the tactics, PCJEWELLER's share prices started to fall. The company announced buybacks to stall the fall, but they conveniently rolled back the scheme as the share prices continued to fall. Further, there are many smaller companies who used bogus but rosy financials to boost the company's valuations and used it as a bait to lure investors and financiers into IPOs, follow on public offers, stake sales in the open market or to raise debts by pledging their company's share.

In early 2017, Lloyd Electric and Engineering Ltd (LEEL) sold its consumer durable (CD) business to Havells for approximately Rs 16 billion and recorded Rs 9.5 billion[1] as exceptional gains. Against this, LEEL's market capitalization was Rs 12 billion then. In 2018, however, the company wrote off Rs 3.1 billion as a one-off exceptional item due to a change in management after the demise of the chairman and managing director, thereby pouring cold water on the minority shareholders' hope to partake into the sale proceeds bounty. It did not stop here. Subsequently, financials started to deteriorate and the management diverted further funds into a number of promoter group entities with unrelated business interests. Minority shareholders started accusing the management of their wrongdoings. The SEBI initiated a probe against the promoters. Perhaps, nothing conclusive may come out of these probes but the wealth destruction is real—LEEL's share price fell by more than 90 per cent.

It is not a new incident and the risk of slump-sale proceeds not reaching minority shareholders is always high. In January 2019, Prabhat Dairy Ltd announced the sale of its flagship dairy business at a much higher price than its enterprise value. The news first pushed the share price higher by 20 per cent, upper circuit in the morning, and by mid-day it fell by 20 per cent, lower circuit, as informed investors realized the risk of misallocation of the sales proceeds. The company's share further slipped by 50 per cent in the next two months. Ironically, the market values these promoters' companies with ongoing business more than when the same business is sold for a significantly higher price. Possibly, the market has learnt that it is a lot easier to misallocate lump sum ideal cash lying in the books than mess up a steady and an ongoing profitable business.

Sterlite Technology Ltd (STRTECH) painted the minority shareholders into a corner in 2015/2016 when it decided to demerge its power business into a separate unlisted entity. The minority shareholders had an option to take Rs 22.5 per share as cash or one shares in an unlisted entity for every five shares held in STRTECH. The cash payment option denies minority shareholders the right to realize the fair market value of the power business, while making the demerged company almost wholly owned by the promoters. Moreover, the cash payment in lieu of a share in the power company seemed low.

Continuing with Sterlite Group, in 2002 Sterlite Industries, after receiving appropriate approvals, initiated a buyback scheme.[2] It mailed cheques worth Rs 150 and bonds worth Rs 50 to minority shareholders when the prevailing market price was Rs 105 per share but the book value was approximately Rs 300. Most interestingly, the offer was binding on all shareholders unless they opted out by signing a form and returning it back to the company, expressing their disapproval. Despite minority shareholders raising their voice against the scheme, the Bombay High Court upheld the scheme. Consequently, post the completion of the offer, the promoter's shareholding rose to 67 per cent from 43 per cent. Later, in 2003, the company name was changed to Vedanta Ltd (VEDL) and was listed in the London Stock Exchange at a premium.

MANAGEMENT: MISLEADING INTO THE TRAP

Purposefully misleading investors by providing overstretched and unachievable guidance is common. The intent is to boost share prices. High prices enable promoters to pledge shares and raise debts, raise equity from institutional investors, sell their stakes in the secondary markets, do right issue and so on. But converting ugly duckling financials into a beautiful swan through window dressing is not common, but not rare either. Tree House Education and Accessories Ltd (TREEHOUSE) operated preschools in India. The company was IPOed in September 2011 and was able to keep its share price artificially high above its IPO price of Rs 153 per share until September 2015. During these four years, the promoter pledged and traded in its shares, and indulged in accounting gimmicks to keep share prices high enough to facilitate frequent fundraising from institutional investors. The money thus raised was possibly misappropriated.

TREEHOUSE's financials are laden with irregularities.[3] While its revenue growth and margins were high, its debtors were uncomfortably higher. From 2013 to 2016, whereas its revenues rose around 90 per cent, its receivables rose eight times. This was followed by a big write-off in 2017. In the fiscal year 2016, TREEHOUSE spent Rs 1.8 billion on furniture, almost equal to that year's revenue, translating into Rs 3 million furniture spent per school. Its employees' median monthly salary was around Rs 4,000 per share—an abysmally low number for preschool teachers. Other irregularities included providing bank guarantees for a personal loan to a director, doubling the auditor's remuneration in a year, booking 33 per cent of total expenses hidden under one miscellaneous expenses line item, extending money to key management persons to buy fixed assets and build the company's offices.

Once the market started to take note of rising receivable and financial irregularities, TREEHOUSE's promoter tried to save the ship by merging it with another more established education company, Zee Learn. A temporary assurance—as soon after the merger announcement, the merger was called off and

TREEHOUSE's share price gradually fell by 98 per cent of its 2011 IPO price.

Manpasand Beverages Ltd (MANPASAND) came out with an IPO in July 2015. It manufactures and sells fruit drinks in India. Mango drinks under the Mango Sip brand is its key product. It also provides various carbonated and non-carbonated fruit drinks (under the Fruits Up brand), blended fruit and vegetables juices. Its revenues rose four times in the last four years leading to the 2015 IPO. The revenues further grew 2.6 times from July 2015 to March 2018. This high growth becomes even more eye-catching as the industry was growing in single digits. On the surface, the company was fast gaining market share from the incumbents who were a few established multinational companies together controlling almost 80 per cent of the mango drinks market. Therefore, it was a great story of a fast-growing young domestic company rapidly gaining market share from the established incumbent players in an oligopolistic industry with meagre industry growth. Sounds like a David vs Goliath gripping play, but even more interesting, here there are a few giant Goliaths and one tiny David beating them all. The promoters of the company claimed that they focused on rural and semi-urban markets which are underserved by larger players. 2Point2 Capital[4] painstakingly surveyed retailers in the rural and semi-urban core markets of MANPASAND and found that the brand was often absent on the shelves and only 10 per cent of the retailers carried MANPASAND's products while ~50 per cent of them stocked Frooti (competitor and market leader in mango drinks). The survey negated MANPASAND's claim that its competitors underserved its core areas. Additionally, the company claims to generate a part of its sales from the Indian Railways/Indian

Railway Catering and Tourism Cooperation (IRCTC) vendors. But ground-level checks reveal that its competitors have similar tie-ups with the IRCTC. Moreover, MANPASAND's Mango Sip is only classified as a 'Category A' supplier by the IRCTC while competitors' products are all classified as 'Category A Special' suppliers. This means that MANPASAND is not allowed to sell its products on premium trains while its competition can.[5] Despite these concerns, the company's share price did not budge. In May 2018, its auditor Deloitte resigned and informed the Ministry of Corporate Affairs that the company has failed to provide crucial information needed to audit the 2018 financials. This was the trigger that led to almost 85 per cent fall in its share price in the next nine months. Falling share prices met deteriorating financials. Revenues remained high but receivables and working capital rose sharply, free cash flow remained negative and capex remained abnormally high. From the fiscal year 2014-18, cumulative operating cash flows was Rs 0.8 billion, just 14.5 per cent of the cumulative EBITDA of Rs 5.4 billion. Working capital rose by Rs 3.5 billion and ate most of the cumulative EBITDA. The cumulative capex during this time was Rs 8.8 billion, leading to a negative free cash flow of Rs 8 billion, which was primarily funded by a cumulative equity infusion of Rs 9.4 billion. Cash flows continued to bleed even though profit and loss statement have been in black. In May 2019, the top management of the company was arrested in a GST fraud.

MANAGEMENT: WE LOVE STORIES

No, I am not talking about Netflix here. I am talking about our greedy nature which makes us fall for investment stories and hypes which promise supernormal future returns. Blinded by greed, we do not question the obvious pitfalls and loopholes in these stories. Indian equity markets are loaded with such examples.

- IT stocks in the late 1990s, such as Satyam, DSQ, Pentamedia among others;
- real estate and infrastructure stocks in 2007;
- education stocks from 2010 onwards;
- NBFC stocks from 2016 to 2017; and
- mid-cap and IPO mania in the last 4 to 6 months of the peak of every bull market.

Some of the common elements in these hypes are listed below:

- Crowded trade, leading to cult type following for the whole sector or theme;
- The more novel the concept, the higher the mania and exuberance in prices.
  - At one end of the spectrum, there are companies whose fundamental and quantitative anchors are missing. Some of these companies have novel concepts or new markets to target. Share prices of such companies are often driven by unquantifiable imaginative stories that have a low probability of materializing. This is precisely why often, a loss-making company is valued more than when it turns profitable. As profit becomes the anchor, the fundamentals start driving the share price and the fundamentals are usually less rosy than exuberant and imaginative stories.
  - At the middle of the spectrum, there are investment trust companies and real estate investment trusts (REITs). These vehicles are valued very efficiently as they have a bondlike structure which allows for near accurate revenue and profit estimation, thereby squeezing out the scope for imagination in equity upside.
  - At the other end of the spectrum, there are niche market leaders with stellar economics that is poorly valued by

the market when their market share approaches a very high number—say more than 50 per cent—while its niche market growth slows down (Accelya Kale Solutions Ltd, for instance). Shrinking available market share to grab and low future market growth means low future growth hope, which consequently results in the company's equity getting poorly valued by the market.

In the words of Richie Norton, 'If you can dream it up, you can team it up.' Story and vision sell well in the bull market.

In the bull market of 2017, story charmers, that is, promoters/manipulators victimized many investors. One such charmer was Shankara Building Products (SHANKARA). SHANKARA engages in the retailing of home improvement and building products in India. Its products range from structural steel products and cement to plywood and kitchen sinks. It was IPOed in March 2017 for Rs 440 per share and was oversubscribed roughly forty-two times. By December 2017, it rose by almost five times to Rs 2,273 per share. For investors, the company ticked all the boxes:

- a 'one-stop-shop' for building material products;
- first mover advantage in India;
- unorganized to organized play;
- benefits from increasing consumer preference for branded products or 'premiumization';
- highly scalable pan-India retail business;
- asset light; and
- quick breakeven at retail store level leading to high RoE.

Forward guidance was ambitious. The 'story' should have sold, and it did. A few brokers issued bullish research reports on the company with lofty price targets. Revenue CAGR was in the low teens due to the fact that even though the retail business was galloping, it was burdened with almost 55 per cent[6] of total revenues coming from slow-moving channel sales and enterprise sales. Nevertheless, the net profit CAGR was expected to grow at 25 per cent plus due to margin expansion.

Investors and share price bought into the hype. Discounted cash flow (DCF) models were stretched, until 2030, like an arrow that would hit a lofty price target. While apparel, footwear and consumer durable segments have seen healthy penetration of organized retailing, building materials was the last bastion of unorganized retailing yet to be conquered. SHANKARA was our warrior to achieve just that. Domestic peer comparison was drawn with established retailing companies such as Aditya Birla Fashion, Trent and even Avenue Supermarts. Parallels were drawn to established international peers trading at 30+ P/E ratios. A successful case study of Home Depot, US and Home Product Center, Thailand was used to justify long-term sustainable high growth in earnings. However, nowhere did people raise red flags on SHANKARA's stabilized net margins in the last ten years at below 2.5 per cent versus high single digit and improving net margin of Home Product Center and Home Depot. Moreover, none of the domestic or international retailing companies had a low stabilized net margin of below 2.5 per cent. SHANKARA's low margin since its inception in the early 2000s, questions the competitive edge which SHANKARA has over its unorganized peers. Low margin has pulled down its RoE from 30 per cent plus in the late 2000s to high single digits by 2019. Lukewarm historical financials were eclipsed by lofty projections. Projections and the story were bought into at face value by investors hungry for 'the next big thing'. Stories hallucinate and delude to such an extent that perpetrators themselves forget that they are overlooking the most crucial point that negates the whole premise.

But with the receding bull market tide from January 2018 onwards, SHANKARA's share price started to correct. The final nail in the coffin came in September 2018 when the management changed its retail strategy and started offering pricing discounts and loyalty benefits to customers, implying that the value add of being a 'one-stop-shop' of building material products to customers is limited. Moreover, its first mover advantage in the organized space is not shielding it from competition from the unorganized market and thereby not resulting in any pricing power over its unorganized peers. This news was not welcomed by the investors, especially since it would mean hurting already low net margins. Consequently, the share price continued to decline and fell 80 per cent plus by February 2019 from its all-time high levels.

BUSINESS: WHEN LEVERAGE MEETS MEDIOCRACY/IGNORANCE

Warren Buffett said, 'When you combine ignorance and leverage, you get some pretty interesting results.' Anil Ambani, Vijay Mallya and many others whose businesses ended up in or close to the bankruptcy camp, would have wished at some point during their downfall to take Buffett's observation a bit seriously.

A bad match causes disaster in the long run, especially when testing times come. This is true not only for failed marriages but also for businesses that fail due to mismatches in the nature of revenue and cost or assets and liabilities. Financial companies have a balance sheet mismatch as they are often funded by short-term liabilities, while their assets, that is, loan books, are mostly long-term in nature. Similarly, many businesses inherently have revenue and cost mismatches. For example, in the hotel industry, costs are mostly fixed but revenues are variable and cyclical. If we add an interest burden to the already high fixed costs, we are just magnifying the mismatch. Other examples of adverse revenue and cost mismatches are commodities and airlines as well as businesses that are prone to competition and disruption. Vijay Mallya's Kingfisher Airlines, Anil Ambani's Reliance Communications (RCOM) and Nair's Hotel Leela Venture (HOTELEELA) nicely fit here. HOTELEELA saw pronounced industrywide downcycles from 2012 to 2018 which lowered occupancy and revenues. But high fixed costs in line with premium service levels and high interest burdens, pushed the company into consistent losses. Similarly, Kingfisher Airlines provided premium service and so had very high fixed costs. That, when coupled with a high interest burden and high oil prices, meant the company never made profits and finally closed down in 2012. Another relevant example is Tata Motor's (TATAMOTORS) acquisition of luxurious Jaguar Land Rovers (JLRs) in 2008 and its subsequent ups and downs—well, more downs than ups! The gist is that a luxury segment of a cyclical industry has even more pronounced cyclicality. Burdening these luxury cyclical segments with a debt-laden balance sheet, result in the necessity of dodging many risks and may not end well. Competition with lower debt and lower fixed cost will always have an advantage.

For most of the indebted promoters in the airline and hotel industry, their business did generate healthy returns. Unfortunately, it was not the traditional return on equity but rather a *return on ego*. However, the ego-inflating businesses eventually reach the bankruptcy camp where promoters lose both the business and the ego.

On the contrary, recently listed Interglobe Aviation (INDIGO) and Lemon Tree Hotels (LEMONTREE) are good examples of how to survive in a tough and cyclical industry by keeping the cost base and debt low and address budget customers where revenue cyclicality is relatively less. INDIGO is cash-rich—a rare example in the aviation industry (New York Stock Exchange [NYSE] listed Southwest Airlines is another example)—and this gives them enough leeway to not only survive tough years but also mop up weak indebted peers over the years and keep getting bigger with time.

Debt-funded RCOM succumbed to the price war and competition waged by Reliance Industry (RELIANCE)-funded Jio. In a price war scenario, a stable funding source is a key competitive advantage that Jio had through RELIANCE's refinery and petrochemical business.

Leverage is not bad per se. Netflix is a prime disruptor which is heavily indebted and is doing fine. Debt suits utilities and REITs as they have almost assured revenues with limited volatility. Thus, the fixed nature of revenue matches fixed cost base that is, the interest burden. Debt is also justified for companies with high competitive advantage. The irony is that such companies often do not need one and are on the contrary, cash-rich and reward shareholders with regular dividends and frequent buybacks.

12

PRINCIPLES—TO BECOME A BETTER INVESTOR

Nothing in life is quite as important as you think it is while you're thinking about it.

—Daniel Kahneman, Israeli-American psychologist

Stocks do not make new highs every single day. Most of the time, we are underwater to our portfolio's high water mark. The BSE sensex index data[1] since 1988 shows that the index made new highs only 6 per cent of the time (or 1 in 16 years). Record market closings are rare! The remainder of the time, the index trades below its all-time highs. Moreover, 37 per cent of the time (or 2 out of 5 years), the drawdown or fall from the all-time highs/peaks was more than 20 per cent. During these times, the market tests us and makes us realize how we missed exiting in the previous peaks. The result is not very different when we look at the S&P 500 index value since 1928. New highs were attained 5 per cent of the time and 20 per cent plus drawdowns were suffered 41 per cent of the time. Globally, new highs in the equity markets are rare. Well, so is spotting live game in a one-week animal safari tour in the wild. If we are lucky to witness a live hunt, we get into action and start clicking multiple pictures. However, during market highs, we rarely sprang into action and sell stocks!

Well, staying within the remit of this chapter and not straying into why we don't sell at peaks, one thing is clear—public equity markets are as much a 'game of mind' as it is of business analysis and valuations. Especially because almost 40 per cent of our time in the market we would be staring at prices that are at least 20 per cent below their past peak. It is a long enough period to test our nerves and conviction and to force us away from long-term buy and hold investing. To navigate through such times, we have to be rational, and rationality requires foresight and worldly wisdom.

To stay rational, I have quite a few principles for myself that I draw upon before making any investments, during market sell-offs and in general. Before we look at them, let us try to answer an obvious question: Why are principles essential? Principles are boundaries that keep our decisions in sync with our values and priorities. A list of well-discovered and intended principles minimizes mistakes and brings us closer to our defined objectives. In normal times, most of these principles sound intuitive. But when placed under market-imposed stress, it is very common to not count on these principles and make mistakes. Consequently, I frequently review these principles in order to keep them fresh in my mind. Lastly, these principles suit me as they cover my weaknesses and raise my chances of doing better in the markets. If you like them, you might want to take these as a first step and build on them in a manner that suits you best.

My principles solely focus on increasing rationality and fall into three main buckets:

1. psychological principles to control the mind;

2. philosophical principles to control the mind; and
3. investment principles to pick stocks with best risk/reward and long-term prospects.

PSYCHOLOGICAL PRINCIPLES—LOWER PATTERNED IRRATIONALITY

Here I follow the legendary investor, Charlie Munger. He has identified twenty-five psychological biases under the heading 'Psychology of Human Misjudgement' and delivered them at a Harvard Law School speech in June 1995.[2] Every investor should check on them regularly in order to reduce mistakes and become wise. I will not repeat them here as they are freely available on the internet and much ink has already been spilled in talking about and explaining them. Nonetheless, I would like to stress that of all those biases, self-deception or denial is particularly interesting and possibly the root cause of most of the investment losses an investor incurs.

PHILOSOPHICAL PRINCIPLES—TO HOLD ON, LET GO

This principle requires long-term investors to check stock prices as infrequently as they can. Yes, it is the hardest thing to do, but it is useful as it is the cause of all self-induced mistakes for a long-term investor. How many of you have observed that in any solo physical or mental activity, not looking at the score has improved your performance? It always happens to me when I read—the number of pages covered in one sitting; swim/run—distance covered; bowling—scores achieved. I can go on, but the point is that in activities where knowledge of past scores does not improve the future scores, knowing the past scores only diverts the mind thereby hurting the final score. Therefore, by not looking at the scorecard, I allow my mind to focus on the current task, resulting in the maximum aggregate score that reflects my true unobstructed potential.

A possible explanation for the above phenomenon is that our mind is like a monkey which jumps from one topic to another for no reason. It needs an anchor. Therefore, when we look at the scoreboard, we place a number in our head. The mind then starts thinking about that number and loses focus on the current task, thereby hurting our performance. In essence, we move away from the present and start focusing on the future outcome, that is, what the final score will be, and so on, thereby hurting the present performance.

Not convinced? Warren Buffett has something to say on this as well, 'Games are won by players who focus on the playing field, not by those whose eyes are glued to the scoreboard.'

Well, it is a lot easier to not look at a game's score than to not look at daily share prices, especially when you have a large concentrated position in a stock that is volatile and underwater.

Reduce the Focus on Output (share prices)

We have to condition ourselves to detach from the habit of regularly checking the movement of the price. The price does not provide any new information but just the demand and supply at that point in time. The demand and supply are influenced by all kinds of buyers: long-term investors, short-term investors, day traders, speculators among others. Of these, day traders, speculators and short-term investors rarely focus on the long-term fundamentals of a company. Thus, the share prices would never entirely reflect the long-term fundamentals of the stock. Additionally, in the long-term investors' camp, there is no consensus on valuations as they see the future of the company differently. Therefore, there are many opaque and non-fundamental variables determining prices that we will never entirely understand but only observe and react to. In this sense, the private equity market is better in price discovery as the buyers and sellers are all mostly long-term investors. Well, it still is not that simple. Even in the private equity market, long-term buyers can be strategic or opportunistic/generalist private equity players. Strategic buyers are known to pay more and crowd out opportunistic private equity players and inhibit the fair price discovery.

The above knowledge is common, but we still look at prices regularly. Right? So, why do we do that and how can we reduce the temptation? Listed below are a few possible ways to decrease this temptation:

Lower your fear

Classic greed and fear make us check the stock prices regularly. I would argue that it is more fear than greed due to our aversion for loss (losses hurt us more than an equivalent amount of profit). Equity markets are volatile. Volatility, if it results in notional losses, incites fear. It makes us check prices regularly. It is either instinctive or is learned by making mistakes. Nevertheless, it is unproductive especially in the markets as it can entice us to do foolish things. Remember the Roman philosopher Seneca the Younger's famous statement: 'Our fears are more numerous than our dangers'. As described in the fifth chapter, the human brain has prefrontal cortex and amygdala. They work as if they are two different brains and compete for control over decision-making. The prefrontal cortex (logical part of the brain) responds in a controlled and analytical fashion while the amygdala (seat of fear and greed) responds with the emotional equivalent of 'shooting from the hip'. When we are analysing the business fundamentals, we use our prefrontal cortex. However, the volatile and uncontrollable share prices induce fear which triggers amygdala-driven emotional decision-making, hijacking analytical decision-making away from the prefrontal cortex. To bring the prefrontal cortex back in control in the investing process, you should:

Know your investments inside out to own your investment decisions

This is one of the most reliable ways to reduce the fear. If you buy on someone else's recommendation, then you will most likely not have the conviction to hold it once the price rises too high or falls significantly.

Be mindful

You need to exercise calm and control over your emotions. To achieve this, try to be aware and mindful of the very moment when the amygdala is triggered. This awareness can assist in transferring control back to the prefrontal cortex and avoid hasty decisions with unintended consequences.

Premeditate

You should forecast the worst-case scenario and our response to it so that if they turn true, we can lower our emotional response (as shock quantum is reduced) and thereby become better in decision-making.

Disassociate

You should try to reduce your association with the outcome. Disassociation is tough but comes with equally superior rewards. It can be achieved by:

- *Enjoying the process:* Consistently strive to evolve into a better investor by focusing on unearthing companies with attractive fundamentals as well as cheap valuations. Moreover, enjoy the hunt. This is important as it breaks the urge to focus too much on the share prices (the outcome). Additionally, enjoying the process will ensure your long presence in the game. This game is quite rewarding monetarily, if done correctly, and the marginal utility of money tapers off quickly. Therefore, the motivation to stick around has to be more than monetary rewards.
- *Staying content:* Lower the attachment to money and fame. By reducing the attachment to these things, you lessen the attachment to share prices and outcomes, thus subconsciously increase the focus on the company fundamentals.
- *Doing charity:* If you don't do charity, start doing it as an experiment, even if in small amounts. Also, lowering materialistic needs can go a long way in reducing our worries about our portfolio returns and can help us shift focus on evolving as a better investor.
- *Decreasing the need to impress:* Refrain from publicly disclosing your favourite stock picks. This prevents you from the chances of shining publicly but equally lessens the need for external validation (i.e., share the price movement of your stocks) to prove your prowess.
- *Embracing personal insignificance:* It will provide the strength to stay calm and neutral in the face of volatile prices, gains and losses. Ask yourself: How much will anything that happens today matter in, say, a thousand years from now?
- *Practising amor fati (love of one's fate):* A Latin phrase that means 'love of one's fate'. It emphasizes accepting that everything happens for a good reason. Such a belief reduces the negative connotation we place on financial losses. Falling

prices should be welcome as they form the base for the next bull run by shaking weak hands and providing the opportunity for long-term investors to enter at attractive prices. Yes, it may lead to notional losses but provides the opportunity for higher tangible future profits on existing and new investments made during such times (The point is to not fear volatility and losses as this fear is more harmful than the loss. This fear induces an investor to convert notional losses into real losses). Alternatively, often investors are wrong and they have to book losses when prices fall. This should also be welcomed as these booked losses are lessons from the market to help us evolve into a better investor. These unfortunate events expose gaps in our investment skills, thereby providing an opportunity to plug them, which, if it remains unplugged, will eventually lead to much bigger losses in the future. So, consider every booked loss as a trigger to improve your investment skill and evolve into a better investor.

Learn to distinguish controllable factors from uncontrollable ones

Rationality guides us to attach to the controllable (business fundamentals) and detach ourselves from the uncontrollable (share prices). In fact, it is a wiser way to control the uncontrollable. So, if you want to monitor something, monitor regularly the company's/competitor's/sector's fundamentals. This will give you more control than following the random price movement. Moreover, it will also help you to decipher the price movement better, that is, determine whether the price movement is fundamentally driven or not. Filter the share prices through the company's fundamentals before taking any action.

The above principles ensure that you are calm and in control during bearish and stressful times. It is important to avoid stupid actions and, more importantly, to benefit from the bearish times by buying more even if our existing portfolio is in red. How you behave during bearish times makes all the difference to your stock returns.

The above observation comes from experiencing a few stock market cycles. Very few have perfected this art and, for me as well, it is a work in progress.

INVESTMENT PRINCIPLES: BE FIRST

In the movie *Margin Call*, John Tuld, the CEO of the investment bank says, 'There are three ways to make a living in this business. Be first, be smarter or cheat.' This underpins my investment principle. Cheating is out of context. I assume I am not smarter. So, I try to be first as much as possible. It is a lot easier than trying to be smart. It ensures that I almost never buy at the peak and so most of my purchases are closer to the bottom than the top.

For any game, it is pertinent to play by its rules. It cannot be truer for investing. The challenge is to understand what the rules are. For the purpose of long-only investment in public companies, we should look for companies that obey the *laws of nature*. Nature is pervasive and is the reality. It does not change for anyone. It rewards adaptation and evolution (survival of the fittest). It is built around rationality and can be brutal. The hyena kills the weakest wildebeest, even if it is a newborn and leaves the rest of the wildebeest group stronger. This act is nature's way of ensuring the fittest survive.

Every bit of nature applies to companies as it does to living beings, including humans. After all, companies are managed by humans for humans (until robots replace CEOs, pun intended). On a daily basis, every corporation struggles to retain and improve its market share exactly as living beings compete over limited resources.

In both cases, the fittest survive and thrive. Moreover, corporation history is generously sprayed with examples of disruption that lead to extinction or adaption/adjustment, thereby pushing the corporations' evolution forward.

Today, technology is disrupting all industries and uprooting incumbents, allowing us an opportunity to learn and gain from this latest adaption process of corporations; for example, driverless transport and electric vehicles; blockchain; renewables and energy storage; robotics (high-frequency algorithm trading; robotic surgery; algorithmic diagnosis); artificial intelligence and the internet of things (across all sectors). Specific global examples of disruptors vs incumbents are Amazon (vs US retail shopping malls), Airbnb (vs hotels), Uber (vs taxis and traditional car companies), Netflix (vs satellite TV), Tesla and BYD Co. (vs traditional car companies). Globally by August 2018 there were 266 unicorns (a unicorn is a privately held startup company valued over US$ 1 bn), and were collectively valued at US$ 861 billion. Nature is as brutal as it is rewarding. The question is, which side are you betting on?

The above perspective of reality and rationality favours growth investing over value investing. Growth investing is investing in companies where future growth is the key investment rationale and which is currently not fully priced in the share price, whereas value investing is investing in companies that are available at a substantial margin of safety (discount) to the fair value of the company without accounting for any future growth. The future growth is disregarded as it remains uncertain. Most of the value stocks are found in sectors where the market perceives limited growth opportunity, that is, sectors with headwinds. On the contrary, growth stocks are seen in sectors supported by tailwinds. To conclude, an investor is rewarded in growth investing through value creation and in value investing through value unlocking. In this sense, growth investing is smarter than value investing as growth investing can create almost infinite value but value investing has finite value unlocking potential. Apparently, if a value stock has strong and reasonably certain growth potential, then it is like sugar on honey—returns will be sweeter.

In addition, value investing requires frequent hunting for new stocks once the existing stocks have exhausted their value unlocking potential. Instead, in growth investing, a few stocks, if identified properly, are sufficient to create value year after year almost in a non-stop fashion. Thus, growth stock requires less decision-making, that is, fewer chances of error once you stumble upon your growth machine. Nature favours growth investing as growing companies exhibit the ability to evolve, adapt and adjust to the current reality. Besides, to grow consistently and sustainably, they must have some competitive advantage. Evidently, you have to be mindful that while investing in growth companies, the price you pay determines future returns irrespective of growth potential. So, paying an excessive price upfront is not wise. Lastly, yes, you should invest in value stocks, but preference should be towards inexpensive growth stocks. In addition, it depends on market conditions. Sometimes, the market throws at us attractively priced growth stocks, sometimes value stocks, sometimes both and sometimes none.

I adhere to the following investment principles (these can be considered as my tough-to-replicate competitive advantages):

Conduct In-depth Independent Research

In-depth research is an art of focus involving curiosity and a long attention span to connect the dots and uncover the reality. It requires independent thinking using data and reasoning. It leaves no scope for assumptions, and everything is stress-tested against solid evidence. It tilts investing odds in your favour, and you effectively become an insider. Investing is a game of being prepared (through independent research and hard work) and patiently waiting for the opportunity. Preparation involves staying mindful to notice signs and things that escape general attention. Leonardo da Vinci said, 'Learn how to see. Realize that everything connects to everything else.' In other words, consider second- and third- order effects as always being present. Nothing exists in isolation. In essence, read the company's and its competitors' communication materials and related periodical journals and connect the dots to extract insights not yet priced in by the market.

Invest with a Long-term Focus

I enjoy analysing and investing in good businesses that offer value or can create value. Nevertheless, both value unlocking and value creation take time, thereby requiring long-term focus. Besides, the market can dupe investors in the short term. Reality emerges in the long term and business find its fair value.

Investing with long-term focus requires aligning to mega trends, which are long-term macro forces defining and shaping the future of the economy and businesses. By aligning to mega trends, you are also aligning with the reality, evolution, nature. Mega trends are a source of long-term and sustainable growth. Once you are invested in companies that exhibit sustainable competitive advantage and are set to benefit from mega trends, practising the buy and hold strategy is rewarding. Unfortunately, experience has taught me that very few companies fit the buy and hold criteria. Most companies' performance starts to deteriorate after a few years of purchase of their stocks no matter how convincing the idea was at the time of purchase. In essence, companies often present a stellar performance for various reasons and attract investors but very few of them are able to sustain the performance. More importantly, it is extremely challenging to know from the onset which company is for the long haul. Therefore, the way it has worked for me is to buy a few of them and get rid of those whose performance, measured across corporate governance, management ability and business fundamentals, start to deteriorate.

Practise Discipline

The cause of straying is greed. Staying contented with what we have is the key to curb greed. To stay content, follow the above philosophical principles. Additionally, the following points should help you to stay grounded:

Stick to core competence

Core competence in investing is a set of proven expertise that allows an investor to see the reality of a certain narrowly defined situation, business, sector or theme and predict the future with reasonable accuracy. Core competence is initially narrow and expands gradually with experience and learning. Sticking to core competence minimizes chances of failure and the speculation element in investing. In this sense, staying within the core competence is akin to picking your battles wisely. This conserves energy to fight the ones where you have the best chance to win. For seasoned investors, the challenge is not to stay within the core competency but to understand when they have trespassed outside of the core competence. This is case-dependent, but when you trespass, your inner voice will tell you that you have.

Learn from your and others' mistakes

Markets humble everyone, but we still make mistakes and lose money. However, when that happens, never forget to connect everything, realize where exactly you went wrong, write it down and hang it on the wall so that you will never forget them. If you forget them, the market will not fail in teaching it to you again. Moreover, there should be a clear pattern to mistakes, and the pattern should guide you to the root cause of those mistakes, thereby providing an opportunity to fix them. Consider mistakes and misfortunes as opportunities to learn from; this attitude will help you develop an anti-fragile personality.

Avoid predicting short-term market movements

Shun derivatives, forex bets, debt, margin and the urge to time the market. In all these situations, short-term market movement mostly influences the outcome—something impossible to predict accurately and consistently. Leverage, margin, trading and derivatives are manna for the knowledgeable and poison for the ignorant. But there is a very thin line between the knowledgeable and the ignorant.

Reduce weak links

Be wise, identify the weak links and kill them. In the financial world, the tendency to speculate is often the root cause of most misery. Well, there are many others. You may do everything right, but one weak link can undo all the good. It is like multiplying by zero, which can undo the entire remaining positives.

Control your hubris when the going is good

Good times is the time when we are most vulnerable. Controlling emotional decisions and reactions during good times should keep you grounded and reduce hubris.

Network

Networking is a two-way street. First, it allows you to test your ideas and seek/reconcile disconfirming views with the smartest people in your field. Networking keeps you in tune with reality and ensures that you see things the way they are and not the way you want to see them. Second, it provides the opportunity to piggyback on others' ideas.

Others

- Be sceptical and seek reality yourself. Do not let your desire or ego keep you from seeing the truth. Do not ignore signs, do not be in denial and take hard decisions early.
- Consider investment as an art. Be situation-/opportunity-dependent and not remain stuck to one investment belief.
- The future will always remain uncertain irrespective of what model you use.
- Judge the management's character appropriately.
- Do not suck your thumb. Be decisive and invest when it is time to act.

I wish I had a shorter list of principles. However, the investing world has many loopholes that the attempt to plug them all keeps extending the list. My key learnings based on my experience can be summarized into three broad categories:

1. Do not suck your thumb and buy when it is time, that is, buy low, when all the signs say so.
2. Let go when it is time, that is, sell high, when all the signs say so.
3. Take hard decisions early on, that is, cut losses by reversing wrong decisions early on.

13

TO FORECAST INDIAN MARKETS, ANALYSE THE US MARKETS

Invisible threads are the strongest ties.

—Friedrich Nietzsche, German philosopher, cultural critic, composer, poet and philologist

If you ask an Indian financial news channel or a stock market expert to cite the factors which explain most of the BSE Sensex 30 movements between 2014 and 2019, you will hear the following reasons:

- Modi mania aka reforms;
- Lower oil prices leading to lower inflation and current account deficit;
- Domestic Systematic Investment Plan in mutual funds;
- Demonetization;
- GST
- National Company Law Tribunal (NCLT);
- Non-banking financial companies (NBFC) crisis;

- Elections;
- Indo-Pakistan border tensions;
- Foreign institutional investor (FII) flows;
- Global liquidity; and
- Global risks such as Brexit or US-China trade war.

People love to complicate things. I bet no one would answer this by providing one reason—the S&P 500. Figure 13.1 would perplex you considerably. From 2003, both the US and India's indices rose due to favourable liquidity conditions. Back then, Brazil, India, China and South Africa (BRICS) were doing the rounds and India made good use of it, generating almost 500 per cent returns from 2003 to 2008. From 2008 onwards, the S&P 500 and BSE Sensex 30 have met the same fate, nicely snuggling up to each other through thick and thin. The correlation from 2008 to early 2019 is a whopping 97 per cent. Need I say more?

Figure 13.1: S&P 500 and BSE Sensex Hugging Each Other

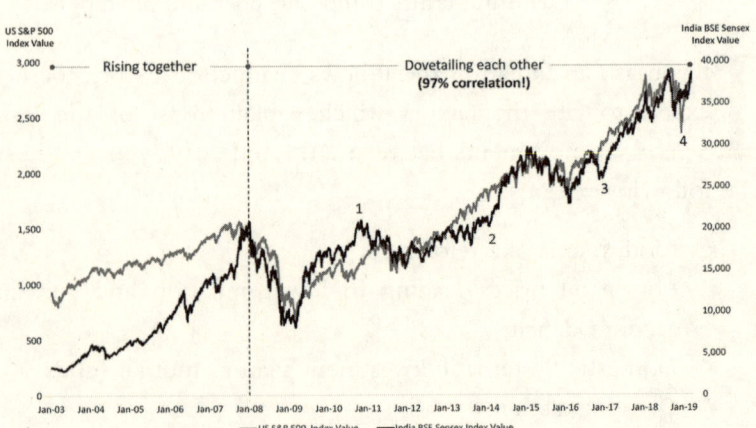

Source: Prepared from Capital IQ data (available at www.capitaliq.com, accessed on 22nd July 2019)

The S&P 500 does not correlate so closely with any other developed and emerging market equity indices. We have globalized our financial markets. Rather, I should say, we have pegged our indices to the S&P 500 as many countries peg their currency to the US dollar.

Figure 13.1 shows how eager the two indices are to snuggle up to each other. Four points (as shown in the figure) are particularly interesting:

Point 1: With the start of quantitative easing in 2009, emerging markets, including India, were the key beneficiary of the risk on trade. By January 2011, India has significantly outperformed S&P 500 and then came the time for a reversal. The BSE Sensex fell to give a bear snuggle to S&P 500.

Point 2: From January 2013 onwards, India underperformed compared to the US markets as the Indian economy was slowing and India was branded as one of the 'fragile five' countries with the rupee taking a severe knock. Then, the Modi government came to power, providing the trigger that pushed the index higher to snuggle S&P 500 again.

Point 3: Demonetization in end-2016 created another uncertainty, leaving the BSE Sensex behind S&P 500. The underperformance did not last long. Soon the Indian BSE Sensex 30 rose swiftly to snuggle S&P 500.

Point 4: Recently, in December 2018, rising US-China trade fears sharply pushed S&P 500 lower by close to 20 per cent. Nevertheless, Indian markets remained relatively resilient. Thus, the S&P 500 reversed course to hug BSE Sensex 30.

Idiosyncratic domestic factors have often separated the two indices but the separation has not been permanent and eventually the indices converge and domestic news flow adjusts accordingly to justify market moves. Indian index movements have often been contrary to domestic investors' expectations, as they do not amply consider the influence of the S&P 500 on the Indian equity index. Consequently, if we have to analyse the Sensex's next move, we are better off analysing the S&P 500 instead of India's domestic economy, corporate earnings or election outcomes. This is a bold statement and a difficult one to digest but remember data does not lie. So, if the US market has benefited significantly from an easy monetary policy, we were not left behind in the party and were fairly dealt with.

Where does this leave the stock pickers, growth hunters and value seekers? The good news is that no matter what happens to the BSE Sensex 30 or the S&P 500, the real booty lies underneath, hidden for investors to dig and unearth. There are around 5,000 listed companies in India and some of them will always provide attractive investment opportunities for various reasons including poor communication with the minority shareholders, tough to understand business models, the market's short-term mindset, cyclical reasons and all the other themes covered in this book.

ACKNOWLEDGMENTS

Every book is a team effort, and this one is no exception. I am very lucky to receive direction from managing partner of ValueQuest Capital LLP and my B-school Professor Sanjay Bakshi. His detailed review and suggestions have enriched the book.

I want to express my gratitude to Samir Arora, founder and fund manager of Helios Capital for his guidance and positioning of the book.

Special thanks to my friends Ankur Jain, Ashish Marwah and Vikash Madhogaria for their eagerness to discuss ideas and provide countless useful suggestions.

Credit is also due to extremely talented Ragini Pachisia, for hours poured in researching various companies covered in this book, checking data and suggesting befitting ideas to improve each of the investment themes.

Finally, I am most grateful to my wife, Richa, for numerous conversations on animal strategies, and for critically reading the manuscript.

All the royalty proceeds of the book will go to Dakshna Foundation, Mohnish Pabrai's philanthropic foundation that prepares gifted poor students for IIT engineering entrance examinations in India.

NOTES

CHAPTER 1

1. Ian Cassel 'Don't Be a Chicken' (available at https://microcapclub.com/2016/11/dont-be-a-chicken/ accessed on 29 May 2019)

CHAPTER 2

1. National Geographic (available at https://www.nationalgeographic.com/animals/mammals/b/blue-wildebeest/, accessed on 29 May 2019)
2. P. Chardonnet *Conservation of the African Lion: Contribution to a Status Survey*. International Foundation for the Conservation of Wildlife, Paris, France, and Conservation Force, Metairie, the US
3. Ibid.
4. Ibid.
5. Ibid.
6. Trading Economics (available at https://tradingeconomics.com/world/population-total-wb-data.html, accessed on 21 July 2019)
7. Trading Economics (available at https://tradingeconomics.com/india/population, accessed on 21 July 2019)
8. Zydus Wellness Limited Annual Report 2018 (available at https://zyduswellness.in/investor/Annual%20Report%2017-18.pdf, accessed on 21 July 2019)
9. Ibid.
10. Ibid.

CHAPTER 3

1. Trevor Carnaby *Beat about the Bush: Mammals and Birds*. Jacana Media, 2013
2. *Economic Times* article 'With 14% rain deficit, this monsoon may end up among worst 3 in 30 years' (available at https://economictimes.indiatimes.com/news/economy/indicators/with-14-rain-deficit-this-monsoon-may-end-up-among-worst-3-in-30-years/articleshow/48949714.cms, accessed on 21 July 2019)
3. Mining.com article 'Thermal coal price hits 10-month high as Chinese buyers snap up cargoes' (available at https://www.mining.com/thermal-coal-price-hits-10-month-high-chinese-buyers-snap-cargoes/3213/, accessed on 21 July 2019)
4. FT.com article 'Call to tackle China's soaring aluminium output' (available at https://www.ft.com/content/2f255636-0b21-11e7-ac5a-903b21361b43, accessed on 21 July 2019)
5. Ibid.
6. GOCL Corporation Ltd, 2013 (available at https://www.bseindia.com/stock-share-price/financials/annualreports/506480/, accessed on 22 July 2019)

CHAPTER 4

1. BBC Planet Earth II Episode 2 (available at https://www.bbcearth.com/modal/episode-two/, accessed on 29 May 2019)
2. Jon P. Costanzo, M. Clara F. do Amaral, Andrew J. Rosendale, Richard E. Lee, Jr., 'Hibernation physiology, freezing adaptation and extreme freeze tolerance in a northern population of the wood frog' in *Journal of Experimental Biology*, 2013 (216): 3461-73. doi: 10.1242/jeb.089342
3. 'Pearls Before Breakfast: Can one of the nation's great musicians cut through the fog of a D.C. rush hour? Let's find out' by Gene Weingarten. *The Washington Post*, 8 April, 2007 (available at https://www.washingtonpost.com/lifestyle/magazine/pearls-before-breakfast-can-one-of-the-nations-great-musicians-cut-through-the-fog-of-a-dc-rush-hour-lets-find-out/2014/09/23/8a6d46da-4331-11e4-b47c-f5889e061e5f_story.html?utm_term=.1eb6005681d4, accessed on 21 July 2019).
4. Mark Everard and Paul Knight *'Britain's Game Fishes: Celebration and Conservation of Salmonids*. Pelagic Publishing, 2013.

5. Social proof bias makes people blindly copy others' actions and behaviour to minimize thinking and adhere to social norms.
6. Consistency bias makes people stick to their past way of doing things even when the facts have changed and warrant a different response. Status quo bias makes people maintain their current or previous decision.
7. Incentives bias makes people repeat the behaviour that is rewarded and shun what is rebuked.
8. The mere association makes people assume that an item has similar qualities to another item in its proximity.
9. Confirmation bias is the tendency to interpret new evidence as confirming an existing belief and ignore evidence that contradicts the belief.
10. 'India Microfinance Crisis brewing' (available at http://rakesh-jhunjhunwala.in/stock_research/wp-content/uploads/India-Microfinance-Sector-Report-19Aug15.pdf, accessed on 22 July 2019)
11. Ibid.
12. Ibid.
13. Ibid.
14. 'Microfinance grows in loan size and urban footprint: EY report' (available at https://www.business-standard.com/article/finance/microfinance-grows-in-loan-size-and-urban-footprint-ey-report-116071900722_1.html, accessed on 17 September 2019)

CHAPTER 5

1. BBC Earth's One Life. Narrated by Daniel Craig, written and directed by Michael Gunton and Martha Holmes (available at http://www.onelifeonscreen.com, accessed on 22 July 2019)
2. Giles Story, 'Anticipating Pain Is Worse Than Feeling It' *Harvard Business Review*, March 2014; 'Fear of Pain May Be Worse Than Pain Itself', *Reuters*, 22 June 1999; Rachel Feltman, 'Worrying you might get hurt is worse than knowing you will, study finds' *Washington*. 29 March 2016.
3. 'Benedetto De Martino, Colin F. Camerer, and Ralph Adolphs, 'Amygdala damage eliminates monetary loss aversion' *Proceedings of the National Academy of Sciences of the United States of America*, 23 February 2010, 107(8): 3788-92 (available at https://doi.org/10.1073/pnas.0910230107, accessed on 22 July 2019)
4. Rohit Potti, 'The Power of Detachment' in *Intelligent Fanatics*; 14 March

2018 (available at https://community.intelligentfanatics.com/t/the-power-of-detachment/422, accessed on 22 July 2019)
5. Catherine Clifford, 'Hedge fund billionaire Ray Dalio: Meditation is 'the single most important reason' for my success' CNBC. 16 March 2018 (available at https://www.cnbc.com/2018/03/16/bridgewater-associates-ray-dalio-meditation-is-key-to-my-success.html, accessed on 22 July 2019)
6. RBI Annual Report dated August 2014 (available at https://www.rbi.org.in/scripts/AnnualReportPublications.aspx?Id=1120, accessed on 22 July 2019)
7. 'Zhou Hongyi makes bold move' (available at https://pandaily.com/zhou-hongyi-makes-bold-move-qihoo-360-returns-chinese-index-via-shell-company/, accessed on 22 July 2019)
8. 'Security Specialist Qihoo Finds Safety in Backdoor Listing' (available at https://www.caixinglobal.com/2017-11-03/security-specialist-qihoo-finds-safety-in-backdoor-listing-101165514.html, accessed on 22 July 2019)

CHAPTER 6

1. Global analysis of the impacts of urbanization on bird and plant diversity reveals key anthropogenic drivers *Proceedings of the Royal Society B*. 281(1780): 2013-3330. doi:10.1098/rspb.2013.3330. Retrieved 30 December 2016
2. 'Migration and remittances factbook 2016' (available at http://siteresources.worldbank.org/INTPROSPECTS/Resources/334934-1199807908806/4549025-1450455807487/Factbookpart1.pdf, accessed on 22 July 2019)
3. Titan Company Limited Annual Reports (available at https://www.titancompany.in/investors/investor-relations/titan-company, accessed on 22 July 2019)
4. Motherson Sumi Systems Limited Annual Reports (available at https://www.motherson.com/annual-reports.html, accessed on 22 July 2019)
5. Eicher Motors Limited Annual Reports (available at https://www.eicher.in/annual-reports, accessed on 22 July 2019)
6. 'India's 150 million-home digital switchover begins' (available at https://www.bbc.com/news/business-20121024, accessed on 17 September 2019)
7. Balaji Telefilms Limited Annual Reports (available at http://www.

balajitelefilms.com/annual-report.php, accessed on 22 July 2019)
8. Wockhardt Limited Annual Reports (available at http://www.wockhardt.com/investor-connect/annual-reports.aspx, accessed on 22 July 2019)
9. Rossell India Limited Annual Reports (available at http://www.rossellindia.com/financials.html, accessed on 23 July 2019)
10: The Rise of Discount Brokers' report by HDFC Securities (available at https://www.hdfcsec.com/hsl.docs/Broking%20-%20Update%20-%20Mar19%20-%20HDFC%20sec-201903191711243793044.pdf, accessed on 23 July 2019)
11. Safari Industries (India) Limited Annual Reports (available at https://www.safaribags.com/investors-relations/annual-reports/, accessed on 23 July 2019)
12. Uniply Industries Annual Reports (available at https://www.uniply.in/investor-relations.html, accessed on 23 July 2019)

CHAPTER 7

1. Benedict G. Hogan, Hanno Hildenbrandt, Nicholas E. Scott-Samuel, Innes C. Cuthill, Charlotte K. Hemelrijk, 'The confusion effect when attacking simulated three-dimensional starling flocks'. 18 January 2017. doi: 10.1098/rsos.160564
2. Anna Azvolinsky, 'Birds of a feather ... track seven neighbors to flock together' for the Office of Engineering Communications, 7 February 2013 (available at https://www.princeton.edu/news/2013/02/07/birds-feather-track-seven-neighbors-flock-together, accessed on 23 July 2019)
3. Amar Singh, Project Coordinator for Foundation for MSME Clusters, *Clusters in India*. Report published in 2010 (available at http://clusterobservatory.in/report/Cluster-in-India.pdf, accessed on 22 July 2019)
4. Navin Fluorine International Limited Annual Reports (available at https://www.nfil.in/investor/annu_reports.html, accessed on 22 July 2019)
5. Sunteck Realty Limited Annual Reports (available at https://www.sunteckindia.com/financials.php, accessed on 22 July 2019)

CHAPTER 8

1. Delta Corp Limited Annual Reports (available at http://www.deltacorp.in/financial.html, accessed on 22 July 2019)
2. Star Cement Limited Annual Reports (available at http://starcement.co.in/?page_id=1341, accessed on 22 July 2019)
3. Titan Company Limited Annual Reports (available at https://www.titancompany.in/investors/investor-relations/financial-information, accessed on 18 September 2019)
4. ITC Limited Annual Reports (available at https://www.itcportal.com/about-itc/shareholder-value/annual-reports/itc-annual-report-2019/pdf/ITC-Report-and-Accounts-2019.pdf, accessed on 18 September 2019)

CHAPTER 9

1. 'Cost of capital—India survey', a report summarizing the survey conducted by E&Y in 2017 among 135 respondents.
2. Prepared from Capital IQ data (available at www.capitaliq.com, accessed on 22 July 2019)
3. Astral Poly Technik Limited Annual Reports (available at https://www.astralpipes.com/investor-relations, accessed on 22 July 2019)
4. Page Industries Limited Annual Reports (available at https://www.jockeyindia.com/annual-reports, accessed on 22 July 2019)
5. Muthoot Capital Services Limited Annual Reports (available at https://muthootcap.com/investors.php#annual-report, accessed on 22 July 2019)

CHAPTER 10

1. Ekaterina Pesheva, 'A cinematic approach to drug resistance' *The Harward Gazette*, dated 8 September, 2016 (available at https://news.harvard.edu/gazette/story/2016/09/a-cinematic-approach-to-drug-resistance/, accessed on 22 July 2019)

CHAPTER 11

1. LEEL Electricals Limited Annual Reports (available at http://www.leelelectric.com/annual_reports.html, accessed on 22 July 2019)
2. Rahul Saraogi, Chief Investment Officer, Atyant Capital Advisors, *Investing in India*.
3. Tree House Education and Accessories Limited Annual Reports (available at https://www.bseindia.com/stock-share-price/financials/annualreports/533540/, accessed on 22 July 2019)
4. *2Point2Capital*, 'The Curious Case of Manpasand Beverages' (available at https://2point2capital.com/blog/index.php/a2016/12/06/the-curious-case-of-manpasand-beverages/, accessed on 22 July 2019)
5. Ibid.
6. Shankara Building Products Limited Annual Reports (available at https://www.bseindia.com/stock-share-price/financials/annualreports/540425/, accessed on 22 July 2019)

CHAPTER 12

1. Prepared from Capital IQ data (available at www.capitaliq.com, accessed on 22nd July 2019)
2. Charlie Munger, 'The Psychology of Human Misjudgment' (available at https://jamesclear.com/great-speeches/psychology-of-human-misjudgment-by-charlie-munger, accessed on 22 July 2019)